BUSINESS &
ADMINISTRATION

dette Watkins

Trimarchi

Majithia

Parton

www.pearsonschoolsandfe.co.uk

✓ Free online support
✓ Useful weblinks
✓ 24 hour online ordering

0845 630 44 44

Part of Pearson

Heinemann is an imprint of Pearson Education Limited, Edinburgh Gate, Harlow, Essex, CM20 2JE.

www.heinemann.co.uk

Heinemann is a registered trademark of Pearson Education Limited

Text © Pearson Education Ltd 2011
Edited by Susan Ross
Designed by Lorraine Inglis
Typeset by Tek-Art
Illustrated by kja-artists.com and Tek-Art
Original illustrations © Pearson Education Ltd 2011
Front cover photograph © Alamy Images/Image Source

The rights of Bernadette Watkins, Karen Trimarchi, Parras Majithia and Nigel Parton to be identified as authors of this work have been asserted by them in accordance with the Copyright, Designs and Patents Act 1988.

First published 2011

14 13 12 11 10
10 9 8 7 6 5 4 3 2 1

British Library Cataloguing in Publication Data
A catalogue record for this book is available from the British Library

ISBN 978 0 435 04690 3

Printed in Spain by Grafos S.A.

There are links to relevant websites in this book. In order to ensure that the links are up to date and that the links work we have made the links available on the accompanying website at www.contentextra.com/businessadmin

Acknowledgements
The publisher would like to thank the following for their kind permission to reproduce their photographs:

(Key: b-bottom; c-centre; l-left; r-right; t-top)

Alamy Images: Aflo Co 55, [apply pictures] 157, David Adamson 175, Jack Sullivan 138, Johnny Grieg LSL 79, Mike Hill 201, Radius images 33, 36, Sami Sarkis 111, Stockbroker MBI 109, Thinkstock 57, **Corbis:** Tammy Hanratty 189; **Getty Images:** AFP 22b, Bloomberg 22t, Stephen Wilkes 74; **Imagestate Media:** Phovoir 206; **iStockphoto:** Andrew J Shearer 7, dsteller 15, Nicole Waring 1; **Masterfile UK Ltd:** 45; **Pearson Education Ltd:** Jules Selmes 103; **Plainpicture Ltd:** Johner 91, 102, 128; **Rex Features:** Terry Harris 121; **Shutterstock.com:** Dean Mitchell 143, 158, Dmitriy Shironosov 149, Film Foto 8, Goodluz 61, iofoto 126, Julien Grondin 185, 195, Michael Jung 117, Monkey Business Images 12, 160, R. Gino Santa Maria 80, Rob Marium 48, Up the banner 183, Yuri Arcurs 151, 153; **SuperStock:** Belinda images 72, Flirt 171; **www.imagesource.com:** Cultura 136

All other images © Pearson Education

The following public sector information has been licensed under the Open Government Licence v1.0:

- p.4 Cover of the HSE booklet
- 60 The population of Great Britain by religion pie chart and table
- 65 extract from the Data Protection Act
- 70 extract

The following materials have been reproduced with kind permission from the following organizations:

- 42 Figure 202.1 Reproduced with kind permission from the CfA
- 44 Table 202.2 Reproduced with kind permission from the CfA
- 57 quote from www.tescoplc.com reproduced with kind permission from Tesco Stores Limited
- 58 quote from www.tescoplc.com reproduced with kind permission from Tesco Stores Limited
- 70 extract reproduced by kind permission of Friends of the Earth
- 71 Reproduced with kind permission from Department for Energy and Climate Change
- 76 With kind permission of the National B2B Centre
- 137 Toyota logo reproduced with kind permission from Toyota(GB)PLC
- 166 Photo approved by Tesco Stores Limited

Every effort has been made to trace the copyright holders and we apologise in advance for any unintentional omissions. We would be pleased to insert the appropriate acknowledgement in any subsequent edition of this publication

Contents

www.contentextra.com/businessadmin

The accompanying website includes the following additional units for this qualification:

Q107 Make and receive telephone calls

Q113 Use occupational and safety guidelines when using keyboards

Q208 Use a diary system

Q211 Provide reception services

Q213 Produce text from notes

Q219 Store and retrieve information

Q220 Archive information

Q221 Use office equipment

Q256 Meet and welcome visitors

SS1   Spreadsheet software

WP1   Word processing software

Plus additional coverage of the Technical Certificate units

How to use this book

This book has been written to help you achieve your NVQ (or SVQ, if you are based in Scotland) Level 2 qualification. It covers the mandatory units and a range of optional units from the 2010 standards, giving you a broad choice of content to match your needs.

Throughout you will find the following learning features.

Key terms

Essential terminology and phrases are explained in clear and accessible language. Where these appear in the book, the first instance of the word appears in **bold** so you know there is a definition nearby.

Activity 3

Use these tasks to apply your knowledge, understanding and skills. These activities will help you to develop your understanding of the underpinning theory and key techniques you will need in your day-to-day working life.

Portfolio task

➡ Links to L01: assessment criterion 1.6

These are tasks that cover grading criteria from the NVQ standards. You can use these tasks to generate evidence for your portfolio. Some portfolio tasks will be supported by downloadable editable forms, which are available from www.contentextra.com/businessadmin.

Functional Skills

You may be taking Functional Skills alongside your NVQ — if so, these are opportunities for you to apply your English, mathematics or ICT skills in a business environment.

✓ Checklist

These features help you to identify important information or steps in a task that need to be completed.

Office life

See how the unit applies to the real world of work, and receive best practice hints and tips for making the most of your time in the workplace.

Doing an Apprenticeship

If you are taking your NVQ as part of an Apprenticeship, you will need to complete a Technical Certificate qualification. This will link to the knowledge and understanding of the NVQ, and these features will tell you about additional information provided on www.contentextra.com/businessadmin to help you complete your Technical Certificate. (See page vi for more information on the website.)

Check your knowledge

At the end of each unit, use this feature to check how well you know the topic and identify any areas you need to recap. The answers for these questions can be found at www.contentextra.com/businessadmin.

About the website

www.contentextra.com/businessadmin

Username: BALevel2

Password: Business

The website accompanying this book will support you in a number of ways as you complete your NVQ.

Welcome to Business & Administration

Home page
FAQ

This website provides additional support to complement the Heinemann NVQ/SVQ Level 2 Business & Administration and NVQ/SVQ Level 3 Business & Administration Candidate Handbooks. Here you will find:

Additional content for book units

Including web links, answers to questions and sample forms to use when completing Portfolio Tasks.

Additional optional units

Full coverage of additional popular units from the NVQ/SVQ, including units at different levels so you can develop a spiky profile.

Technical Certificate units

Doing an Apprenticeship? Use the dedicated Technical Certificate units to revise for your on-screen assessment or develop your knowledge and understanding to help you produce a portfolio.

Getting started

Log into the website using the user name and log-in details on p.vi of the book, and select the content you want to see from the left-hand menu.

About | Privacy Policy | Terms and Conditions | Contact Us | © Copyright 2011 Pearson Education Ltd

Extra free support

For the units covered in this book, you will find the following additional support materials:

- downloadable forms and templates for portfolio tasks
- answers to 'Check your understanding' questions
- links to useful websites for further reading.

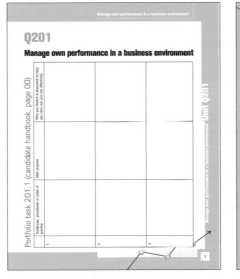

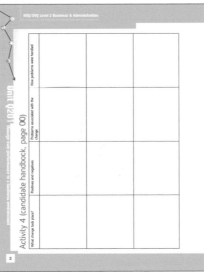

Additional free units

The website contains additional units, not covered in the book, providing you with a broader choice of units to better suit your needs. Each unit is available as a downloadable PDF for your personal use, and also includes answers, template forms and links to useful websites.

The additional units on the website are:

- Q107: Make and receive telephone calls
- Q113: Use occupational and safely guidelines when using keyboards
- Q208: Use a diary system
- Q211: Provide reception services
- Q213: Produce text from notes
- Q219: Store and retrieve information
- Q220: Archive information
- Q221: Use office equipment
- Q256: Meet and welcome visitors
- SS1: Spreadsheet software
- WP1: Word processing software

Bonus support for Apprentices

If you are taking the NVQ as part of an Apprenticeship, you will also be taking a Technical Certificate. This qualification assesses the knowledge and understanding that underpins the NVQ.

The website includes concise unit-by-unit summaries of the key knowledge and understanding you need to complete your Technical Certificate — perfect for revising for on-screen assessment.

Unit TC2-1   Principles of personal responsibilities and working in a business environment

Introduction

This unit provides a brief summary of the knowledge which you will need in order to successfully complete unit TC201 of the Technical Certificate element of your Apprenticeship.

You will begin by looking at employer and employee rights and responsibilities, as well as health, safety and security issues in the workplace. These issues are all central to ensuring that you carry out your duties correctly and you comply with all relevant laws and company procedures.

Communication is an important issue at work and you will investigate this, along with how to communicate effectively at work. You will go on to consider the wider issue of how to work well with colleagues and support others.

Planning your work to best effect is central to being effective in your work. You will look at this issue, as well as deciding how to relay your progress on work tasks to others in the most efficient manner.

Improving your own performance is an important aspect of progressing well at work. You will investigate how you can achieve this to ensure you are seen as having potential for future career advancement.

Finally, you will look into the types of problems which may occur in the workplace and at how and when you should refer problems to others to deal with.

What you will learn:

- Know the employment rights and responsibilities of the employee and employer
- Understand the purpose of health, safety and security procedures in a business environment
- Understand how to communicate effectively with others
- Understand how to work with and support colleagues
- Know how to plan own work and be accountable to others
- Understand the purpose of improving own performance in a business environment and how to do so
- Understand the types of problems that may occur in a business

1

Unit Q201

Manage own performance in a business environment

What you will learn

- Understand how to plan work and be accountable to others
- Understand how to behave in a way that supports effective working
- Be able to plan and be responsible for own work, supported by others
- Behave in a way that supports effective working

Introduction

In this unit, you will learn about how you can best manage your performance at work in order to support the effective working of your team, department and organisation.

You will investigate methods of work planning that will help you to get the most out of your working day as well as making sure you achieve your work goals to the best of your ability.

Responsibility is an important issue in the workplace. You will look at what this means for you and how you can take responsibility for your own work. You will also consider the issue of accountability, and what this means for you as an employee.

In particular, this unit focuses on the issue of behaviour at work and on the importance of professionalism in the workplace when working with others. The way in which you behave has a direct impact on your colleagues and, for this reason, you will examine ways in which you can behave to best support the effective working of the team. This is an important skill, not only for your current job, but for your future career success.

Doing an Apprenticeship?

If you are taking your NVQ as part of an Apprenticeship, you will find that the knowledge and understanding for this unit links to your Technical Certificate. Go to www.contentextra.com/businessadmin to find summaries of the Technical Certificate units.

How to plan work and be accountable to others

In this section, you will learn how to plan your work in order to ensure you complete all your tasks, both on time and to a high standard. You will also investigate target setting and ways to plan your work to meet important **deadlines**.

You will look at the importance of keeping your colleagues updated on your work progress, who you should turn to for help when things go wrong and, finally, you will explore how to learn from mistakes as this is a key method of self-improvement.

Guidelines, procedures and codes of practice at work

Guidelines, procedures and codes of practice that relate to your work are very important as each of them gives you essential information on how to perform your job effectively and safely. By failing to follow guidelines, procedures and codes of practice, you could potentially harm yourself or others and you might also overlook **employment legislation** which could cause problems for the business.

Key terms

Deadline – the date by which a task must be done. Missing a deadline can affect the way a business runs.

Employment legislation – special laws relating to work.

Guidelines

Guidelines are generally informal and can cover things like answering the phone, working the fax machine (see Figure 201.1), sending an email request to a supplier, or writing a report.

Businesses provide guidelines to their staff for many areas of their work in order to help them carry out their tasks in the best and safest way and to avoid errors. Providing guidelines is a good way to make sure activities are carried out effectively and in the same way by everyone in the team, department and the organisation.

When employees follow guidelines customers often gain a better impression of a business since this will help them to know the level of service they can expect. This is particularly important when working in reception, for example.

Guidelines for sending a fax

1. Always use a cover sheet and ensure it is filled in correctly.

2. Only send information that is clear.

3. Keep the content of the fax short and to the point.

4. Avoid sending personal or confidential information.

5. Always obtain a fax-sent receipt as proof of sending and keep this until you know the recipient has confirmed receipt.

Figure 201.1: *How do you think these guidelines for sending a fax will help employees do their jobs more effectively?*

Procedures

Businesses usually have procedures for major issues that could have serious consequences for an employee – and the business – if not handled correctly.

Procedures are more formal than guidelines and cover such issues as:

- fire drills (see Figure 201.2)
- customer complaints
- reporting of accidents at work
- reporting employee absence from work.

A procedure consists of a set of clear, straightforward instructions telling the employee what to do in certain situations. This is valuable as it means everyone will follow a uniform approach, with a controlled set of actions and events, instead of doing things their own way. Clear procedures also can help a business keep within its legal requirements.

Fire Procedure

If you hear the fire alarm:

- don't panic
- leave the building by the nearest exit in a calm manner
- go to the meeting point
- do not re-enter the building until you have been informed it is safe to do so.

If you discover a fire:

- don't panic
- do not try to tackle the fire yourself
- activate the alarm by breaking the glass on the nearest alarm panel
- follow the instructions on leaving the building above.

Figure 201.2: *Why do you think it is so important to have a formal procedure in the event of a fire?*

Key term

Industry body – organisation set up to monitor and regulate the activities of its members. For example, the UK's regional water companies are regulated by the Office of Water Services (Ofwat), which ensures that they act in accordance with its rules and regulations on water quality and prices.

What does the HSE code of practice on first aid at work mean for your workplace?

Codes of practice

Codes of practice are widespread in business and can be produced either by a business or an **industry body**. They set out minimum standards for customer service, quality assurance and respect for privacy of personal data that customers can expect from the business or industry. Where an industry body sets a voluntary code, businesses do not need to sign up to it. However, it shows that they are a reputable business if they do.

Activity 1

Find out which codes of practice are relevant to your job and organisation. Ask colleagues and managers to help you identify these.

The Health and Safety Executive (HSE) in the UK has published a code of practice for first aid in the workplace. It tells employers what they need to do and describes the first aid provision required for their staff. For a link to the HSE website, please visit www.contentextra.com/businessadmin

Portfolio task 201.1 ➔ Links to LO1: assessment criterion 1.1

Find and list three of the guidelines, procedures or codes of practice which relate to your job. Think of all of the tasks which you carry out each day. Which of these have you received training for? Locate any documents which you were given at this time as they may contain important information on guidelines or procedures.

Ask your line manager to help you locate information on any other guidelines, procedures or codes of practice which relate to your job.

For each one that you choose, say what it is for and why you think it is important to help you carry out your job effectively. The table below may help you to collect all of the information to complete this portfolio task.

Guidelines, procedures or codes of practice	Main purpose	Why you think it is important to help you carry out your job effectively
1		

A version of this table, ready for you to complete, is available to download from www.contentextra.com/businessadmin

Planning work and being accountable to others

There is a well-known saying often used in business, 'Failing to plan is planning to fail.' It means that if you do not plan your work properly, you will not succeed in making the best of your working day and will not achieve the best results. Let's take a closer look at what this means in practice.

Why do I need to plan my work?

Planning your work is a vital part of your job. At the planning stage, you will need to:

- consider all of the tasks that you need to complete
- estimate the time needed to complete each one
- work out which tasks need to be completed before others can be started
- list the deadlines by which the tasks need to be completed
- identify any urgent tasks which you need to attend to
- identify any tasks where you will need help from someone else.

By taking a little time at the beginning of the day to plan your work, you will dramatically improve your **productivity** and work **efficiency** and you will also have an at-a-glance checklist of your tasks for the day, which you can then tick off as you complete each one. This will help you to monitor your own progress.

Key terms

Productivity – the rate at which a person works. The more productive you are, the more you will achieve.

Efficiency – the speed and the quality of work. A task completed efficiently is one that is done quickly and to a good standard.

✓ Checklist

Planning your work

When planning out your work for the day, remember to include the following information for each task.

- What is the deadline for completing the task?

- How much time will you need to complete the task?

- Do you require help from another person to complete the task?

- Is the task urgent?

- When will you start the task?

Key terms

Job description – a list of the key tasks you are responsible for and the person you report to, usually your line manager. A job description is provided to employees when starting a new job.

Accountable – to be responsible for something. You are also accountable to someone for completing your work tasks, usually your line manager.

Line manager – the person to whom you report at work. Your line manager is also the person who gives you your work tasks and sets the deadlines for you to work to.

Accountability

At work, you will have a **job description** that sets out the duties for which you are responsible, or **accountable**. For example, an administrative assistant may be responsible for ensuring that the minutes of team meetings are accurately taken and then circulated to the whole team afterwards. This means that the administrative assistant is accountable for these tasks. They will also be directly accountable to their **line manager** for making sure these tasks are completed on time and without errors.

Being accountable at work is important as it will help you to meet the expectations that people have of you. If you fail to complete your tasks properly, you will have to explain the reasons why to your line manager.

Activity 2

For your job role, you need to understand the key tasks for which you are responsible, or accountable. Make a list of them. Next to each task, make a note of the person to whom you are accountable. This is usually your line manager but it could also be someone from another department, depending on the task.

Portfolio task 201.2 → Links to LO1: assessment criterion 1.2

1 Produce a short written summary which explains the reasons why you think it is important to plan your work.

2 Give three examples of work tasks that you are doing at the moment and show how you have planned to complete each of these by the deadline.

3 Outline what you understand by the term 'accountable'. Who are you accountable to for your work?

Agreeing realistic targets for work

At work, many tasks will be competing for your attention. You may be asked to complete certain tasks immediately – if you already have a full schedule for the day, it may not be possible to do this. For this reason, you must always set and agree **realistic targets** for completion of work tasks. Furthermore, you should make a point of getting this agreed by email, so that you have a record of the discussion and of the agreed completion date.

Why do you think it is important to set realistic targets for your work?

Purpose of realistic targets

Agreeing realistic targets will:

● ensure you do not become overloaded with work that you cannot complete

● allow you the time to complete your allocated work in a proper manner

● avoid you suffering from anxiety due to an overload of tasks

● prevent errors occurring due to excessive **workload**

● make sure that deadlines are met, and the work is completed to a high standard.

Unrealistic targets are likely to end in work not completed properly, staff becoming unhappy and errors being made. This can lead to work needing to be redone or corrected, which requires additional time and expense. As you can see, it is in nobody's interest to have unrealistic work targets.

Benefits of realistic targets

Below are the benefits of working to realistic targets.

● You will have the right amount of time to complete your work.

● You will produce better results and be able to work to a high standard.

● You will have enough time to look over what you have done and see if you can make improvements.

Key terms

Realistic target – a task that can be completed within the time given.

Workload – the tasks which you need to complete.

Portfolio task 201.3

→ Links to LO1: assessment criterion 1.3

Write a short paragraph which explains the purpose and benefits of agreeing realistic targets for work.

Be prepared also to take part in a discussion about your written answer with your assessor. Ensure you are able to give reasons for your answers.

Functional Skills

English: Speaking, listening and communication

If you take part in a professional discussion with your assessor, you may be able to count it as evidence towards Level 2 Functional English: Speaking, listening and communication through taking part in formal and informal discussions/exchanges.

How to agree realistic targets

We have seen why it is important to agree realistic work targets. Now you will find out how to do this in practice. Figure 201.3 shows the steps that you need to follow in order to agree realistic targets for work.

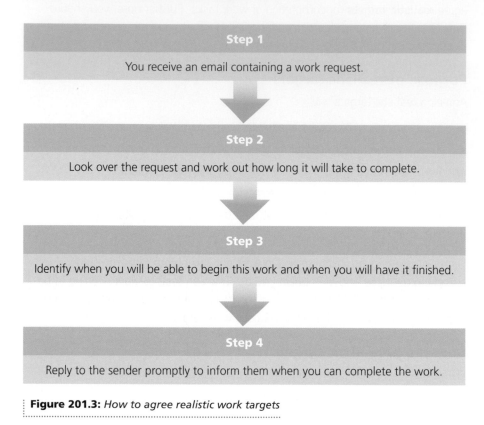

Step 1

You receive an email containing a work request.

Step 2

Look over the request and work out how long it will take to complete.

Step 3

Identify when you will be able to begin this work and when you will have it finished.

Step 4

Reply to the sender promptly to inform them when you can complete the work.

Figure 201.3: *How to agree realistic work targets*

Let's take a look at how this process works in practice.

Step 1: It is Monday lunchtime. You receive an email from your line manager asking you to type up a 4000 word report, make 50 copies and send it out to 50 people. Your line manager would like this done by tomorrow.

Step 2: You look over the request and estimate that the task will take you 4–5 hours to complete.

Step 3: Next, look at your current workload. Identify when you will be able to begin this new work. You can work out from this when you will have it finished. You see that you cannot begin this new work until tomorrow afternoon.

Step 4: Reply to the sender, acknowledging receipt of the request. Inform them of the earliest start date and completion date which you can manage. Suggest that if this is going to be a problem, then perhaps you can negotiate stopping work on your current project to allow you to complete this new request.

✓ Checklist

Agreeing targets

When agreeing work targets with others, remember to:

- reply to their requests promptly

- inform them immediately if you cannot meet the deadline, explaining politely the reasons for this

- offer an alternative deadline if you cannot meet the suggested one

- let them know if, while carrying out the task, something holds you up and the deadline needs to be reset

- act politely and professionally at all times.

Portfolio task 201.4
➜ Links to LO1: assessment criterion 1.4

Write a short report which explains how to agree realistic work targets. Remember to use examples from your own job. Describe two tasks or projects for which you had to agree work targets and say how you went about agreeing realistic targets to complete them.

Did you come across any problems with others during this process? If so, how did you manage this?

If you have not yet had to agree realistic work targets with anyone at work, write about how you think you would go about this.

Functional Skills

English: Writing

If you take care to format your report for portfolio task 201.4 in a professional and business-like manner, with headings and subheadings, check you have used correct spelling and grammar and then print out the final corrected version, you may be able to count it as evidence towards Level 2 Functional English: Writing.

Ways of planning work to meet agreed deadlines

Where there are several tasks that all need to be completed in a short time, planning your work to make sure agreed deadlines are met can be complicated. To help you to plan and arrange your work, you will need to use a planning tool, either a paper-based diary on your desk or an electronic diary system on your computer.

Whichever planning method you prefer, start by blocking out times that are set aside for meetings, team briefings, or day release, as you will not be able to complete any work tasks during these times.

Would you prefer to use an electronic or a paper-based diary to plan your work?

Next, compile a 'To do' list for the week. This should list all of the work that you have been asked to do, along with your own routine daily and weekly work tasks. Make sure you list the deadline next to each task as this is essential information that will enable you to plan your schedule of work for the week.

Now prioritise your work — place tasks in order of importance to make sure the most urgent work gets done first. Work requests from senior managers will have to be prioritised above those from junior colleagues.

Finally, allocate dates and times to tasks. Once you have done this, you will have created your work schedule for the week.

Planning your work

Figure 201.4 shows the steps you will need to follow when planning your work to meet agreed deadlines.

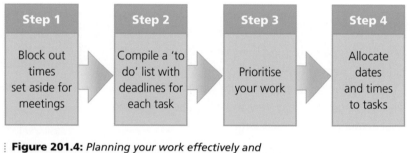

Figure 201.4: *Planning your work effectively and prioritising tasks will help you meet deadlines*

Portfolio task 201.5 → Links to L01: assessment criterion 1.5

Write a short summary which describes ways in which you go about planning work to meet agreed deadlines.

You may like to use the steps outlined in the section above as a basis for your answer. It may help if you use some of your own work as examples and show how you scheduled them into your working week.

Remember to mention which type of diary system you use and why. You should also include examples of any problems you encountered when planning your work and how you dealt with them.

Office life

Dean's story

My name is Dean Hunter. I'm 24 and have been working as an administrative assistant for Excelsior Merchandise for 18 months. During that time, the company has grown significantly and we have taken on a large number of new sales staff, who are not office based, as they are always out on the road travelling long distances to visit customers. I am the central contact point for them, and it is my job to keep track of their appointments during the working day and to process the orders which they send in from customers.

All of this tracking and order processing is carried out manually using a paper-based system. This worked fine when we only had four sales reps. However, we now have a sales force of 20, and keeping abreast of all the paperwork which is generated every day is becoming almost impossible, with the result that problems are beginning to arise with missed appointments, lost order sheets, and ultimately lost business for the company.

Ask the expert

Q I have to look after the diary management for a large number of sales reps. I also have to process the orders which they send in. I am overloaded with the paperwork which this generates and am starting to worry, as orders are being lost due to missing paperwork.

A In such a situation, it would help you to move to an electronic system. This will offer a much easier way for you to ensure accuracy in administration. Electronic diary systems enable you to run a calendar service and to share calendars, so you can keep on top of the sales reps' schedules. Also, by equipping your sales team with laptops, they could then email in all customer orders, which you can then process electronically.

Top tips

There are advantages and disadvantages to both paper-based and electronic diary systems. However, when there are many staff to administer, and a large volume of paperwork being generated, it is often better to use an electronic diary system. First, for the management of the sales reps' appointments, an electronic calendar system will be much easier to administer than a paper version. Secondly, for the processing of orders, using an electronic system will allow for a much more streamlined process and will eliminate the possibility of lost orders as a result of missing paperwork.

Why do you think it is important to keep people informed of your progress on tasks you are completing for them?

Key term

External client – a customer who works for another organisation.

Keeping other people informed about progress

When working in a business administrative role, you are likely to carry out tasks and provide essential support for a number of people — including colleagues, senior managers and company directors — who may be in different offices or departments, or even different geographic locations. They all trust you to complete their work for them and rely on you for efficient service.

It is therefore very important to keep them informed about your progress on tasks. It gives them reassurance and peace of mind to know everything is proceeding as planned. It also helps them to plan if, for whatever reason, you are unable to complete the task to the given deadline. This is especially important where it is an urgent or important piece of work, perhaps for a senior manager or an **external client**.

Keeping people informed of progress saves them from having to contact you for information. This can be frustrating both for them and for you. By taking the initiative — contacting people before they contact you — you are likely to receive fewer emails and phone calls, which will allow you to continue, uninterrupted, with your work.

Activity 3

You may find it helpful to have a set paragraph of text prepared, which you can use in emails to update people on your progress. Similarly, you could have a paragraph for those occasions where you need to reschedule deadlines. This will save you from typing out the same thing over again.

Draft an email for this purpose and try using it to update your colleagues with your progress on different tasks.

Examples of progress reports to colleagues

When communicating your progress on projects, your phone call or email should be polite, clear and give the recipient the information they need in order for them to feel at ease and confident that you are working as planned on their task. Figure 201.5 shows an example of such an email.

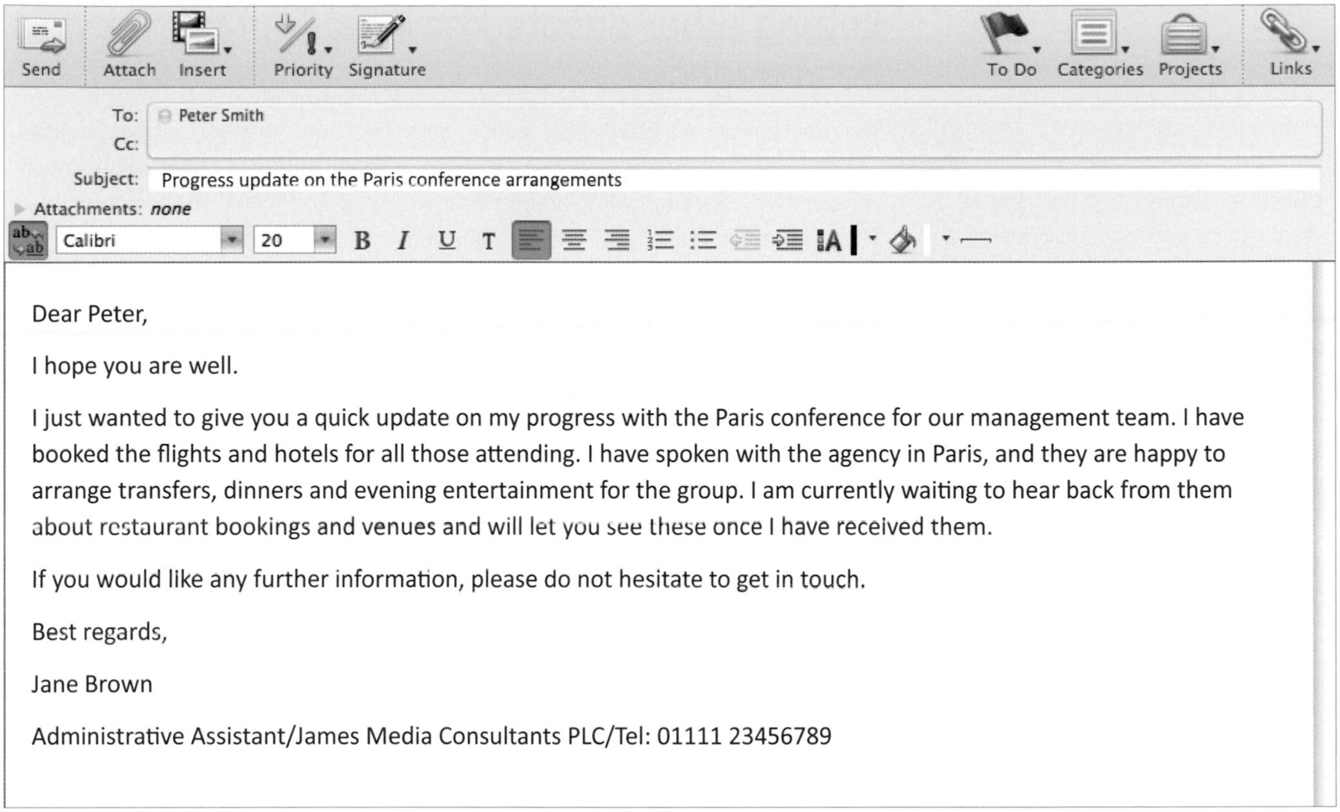

| Send | Attach | Insert | Priority | Signature | | To Do | Categories | Projects | Links |

To: ⊜ Peter Smith
Cc:

Subject: Progress update on the Paris conference arrangements
▶ Attachments: *none*

| Calibri | 20 | **B** *I* U T | ≡ ≡ ≡ | ⋮≡ ⋮≡ ⋵ ⋵ | |A| ⬩ ◈ ⬩ — |

Dear Peter,

I hope you are well.

I just wanted to give you a quick update on my progress with the Paris conference for our management team. I have booked the flights and hotels for all those attending. I have spoken with the agency in Paris, and they are happy to arrange transfers, dinners and evening entertainment for the group. I am currently waiting to hear back from them about restaurant bookings and venues and will let you see these once I have received them.

If you would like any further information, please do not hesitate to get in touch.

Best regards,

Jane Brown

Administrative Assistant/James Media Consultants PLC/Tel: 01111 23456789

Figure 201.5: *How do you think this progress update helps other people plan their work?*

Portfolio task 201.6

→ Links to LO1: assessment criterion 1.6

Write a short report which explains the purpose of keeping other people informed about your progress with work.

Remember to include the email which you produced in Activity 3 above.

Make sure you talk about your current job and use two examples from it to show how you keep people at work informed about your progress with tasks. Also include any examples of where you had problems in this respect, and say what you did to deal with them.

Functional Skills

English: Writing

You may be able to count your piece of work from portfolio task 201:6 as evidence towards Level 2 Functional English: Writing

Take care to draft suitable text for your report and format it well. Ask your assessor for guidance on checking that your work is as error free as possible.

Remember to check that you have used correct spelling and grammar in your email and then print out the final corrected version.

Letting other people know work plans need to be changed

You may sometimes have more work to complete than time will allow. Priorities can change, new urgent work comes along, a major job for a **client** might mean you suddenly have to switch around your workload and focus on something else. There are many reasons why work plans may need to be changed.

All of this will mean that you have to look again very carefully at what you had agreed to complete for people. If your original agreed deadline now has to be changed, it is vital that you inform whoever gave you the work as soon as you can. Waiting until the last minute, or worse, forgetting to let people know, will cause frustration and upset.

Purpose of letting other people know

There are a number of reasons why you need to let people know if work plans need to be changed.

- They may have already promised to give your completed work to an important client by a certain date. In this situation, the more notice you can give of the delay, the least damage will be done to the **client relationship**.

- They may need your completed work for another meeting, and may then have to reschedule this meeting to wait for your delayed work, or else find another colleague to help get it done on time.

- If someone is expecting work completed from you at a certain time, a change of plan may also affect their other work commitments. They need to be informed of any changes that will impact on their other work so that they can make alternative arrangements.

Benefits of letting other people know

Below are the key benefits of letting people know when work plans need to be changed.

- They will be able to take whatever action is necessary to make allowances for this change.

- They have the time to see if they can find someone else to complete the work for them.

- If these changes affect other people in the business, they can be made aware of the change ahead of time, minimising any disruption.

- It is good professional practice to inform people if you have to change plans that were previously agreed with them, as it shows integrity (honesty) and initiative.

Portfolio task 201.7   → Links to LO1: assessment criterion 1.7

Write a brief summary which explains the purpose and benefits of letting other people know when work plans need to be changed.

You may find it useful to re-read the section above to help you plan your answer.

If you are asked to take part in a professional discussion about this task with your assessor, include examples from your own job and show what happened when you let people know when plans had to be changed. If you came across any problems during this process, include these as well, along with an explanation of how you dealt with them.

Types of problems that may occur during work

There are many different types of problems that can occur at work and that might prevent us from completing tasks as planned. Problems can arise as a result of:

- technology failures
- equipment failures
- administrative errors
- misunderstandings between different departments.

Each can cause delays and sometimes frustration to all affected by them.

Technology failures

Examples of technology failure include no Internet connection, your PC crashing or the software you are using stopping working, both of which may cause you to lose your work. These problems can hold up your work and delay completion of your projects. In order to reduce their impact, you should save your work regularly and keep back-up copies of documents.

Equipment failures

When printers, scanners, binders, laminators or fax machines break down they can cause frustrating delays to your work, especially if you are trying to prepare material for an important meeting.

Do you know who to tell when you have a technical problem?

Administrative errors

Administrative errors, such as accidentally inserting an extra zero into a quoted price for a customer or misspelling an important client's name, could lose customers for the business. These types of mistake are usually the result of human error and can often be prevented by carefully checking your work.

Misunderstandings between different departments

Misunderstandings can occur about such things as delivery dates, **discounted prices** or supply order quantities and, as a result, may lead to extra costs for a business.

Certain problems, such as administrative errors, can be prevented by being careful with your work. Misunderstandings between departments about supply order quantities can be prevented by having clearer communications between departments.

However, other problems may be beyond human control such as lack of an Internet connection or a PC crashing. The best you can do is to have a back-up plan for such circumstances. Suitable back-up plans in this situation might include having a spare laptop and a mobile broadband USB stick (a dongle) to hand. These items can usually be ordered from the IT department, if you have one, or the office manager.

> **Key term**
>
> **Discounted price –** where the original price of an item has been lowered.

Portfolio task 201.8 → Links to LO1: assessment criterion 1.8

Write short notes which describe three types of problems that may occur during work.

You may find it useful to re-read the section above to help you plan your answer.

If you are asked to take part in a professional discussion about this task with your assessor, remember to tell them about examples from your own job and say whether and how any of these problems could be prevented.

Getting help to resolve problems

When things go wrong at work, there are usually a few options for getting some help to resolve them. The help you need will depend on the type of problem. For each of the problems described in the previous section, there will be a different solution. Look at the examples given in Table 201.1 and see if you can think of any more possible solutions to add to it.

Table 201.1: Solving common problems

Type of problem	Possible solutions
Technology failures (Internet connection failure, PC crash)	Contact your IT technician or help desk.
Equipment failures (printers, scanners, binders, laminators, fax machines)	Find out who is responsible for servicing these pieces of equipment and contact them to report the problem.
Administrative errors (spelling errors in reports and documents)	Ask for help from another colleague by getting them to proofread your reports and documents before they are sent out.
Misunderstandings between different departments	Ask your manager to require that all staff double-check requests from other departments by asking for confirmation of dates, quantities, and so on, to minimise errors.

✔ Checklist

Using the spell-checker

When using your computer's spell-checker remember that it will not pick up all mistakes. For example, 'their' and 'there' used incorrectly will not be flagged up as they are both correctly spelt words in their own right.

Portfolio task 201.9   ➡ Links to LO1: assessment criterion 1.9

Write a short set of instructions which can be given to new members of staff in your team describing ways of getting help to resolve three types of problems. Think about how you would do this in your current job. List the different options which are open to you.

Which types of problem would you refer to your line manager and for which would you request help from somewhere else?

Recognising and learning from mistakes

It is a fact of life that we all make mistakes. Some are minor and will be of little or no consequence, while others may have far-reaching consequences for many people.

The most important thing here is to make sure that you recognise when you have made a mistake and learn from it. As a result, you will be more fully equipped to make better decisions when faced with a similar situation in the future and you will be less likely to repeat the mistake. If you fail to recognise when you have made a mistake, you cannot learn from it.

But how do you recognise a mistake? The best way is to reflect on your work and activities afterwards. Quite often, this will help you to see things differently than you did at the time.

> ### ✓ Checklist
>
> **Reflecting on mistakes**
>
> Remember, to recognise a mistake, reflect on the situation. To make sure you learn from a mistake, think about how you could do things differently the next time you are in a similar situation.

> **Portfolio task 201.10**   → Links to L01: assessment criterion 1.10
>
> Write a short paragraph which outlines the purpose of recognising and learning from your mistakes. You also need to include a section which describes the benefits of recognising and learning from mistakes.
>
> It may be helpful to describe an example from your own work. Say what the mistake was, how you recognised it and how you learned from it. Remember to say what you would do differently in this situation the next time.

Key terms

Annual performance review – a meeting between an employee and their manager to discuss the employee's work performance over the past year and set work-related targets for the forthcoming year.

Formal meeting – usually involves following a prepared set of questions. The meeting may include more senior managers and opportunities to speak freely will probably be limited.

Informal meeting – often takes the form of a general discussion about how well the employee has done in their work. The employee is likely to have freedom to express their thoughts and feelings openly.

Career progression – the jobs you will move on to later in your working life.

How to behave in a way that supports effective working

This section looks at the importance of your behaviour in the workplace and why you need to set high standards for yourself and your work. You will also think about the issue of adapting to change in the workplace and how to deal with this. Finally, you will learn why it is important to treat others with respect and consideration and at ways of behaving to achieve this.

Agreeing and setting high standards for your work

You will discuss and agree with your line manager the work standards that will be expected of you. This often takes place at an **annual performance review**, which can be a **formal** or **informal meeting**, depending on the circumstances.

Purpose of setting standards

High standards are something that you should aim to achieve at work, in order to show that you are capable and hard working, as well as to demonstrate your potential for future **career progression**.

People who set low standards for themselves often become bored quickly and have little interest in their work. High standards present a challenge — they require a person to work hard and make an effort to achieve them. This is why the achievement of high standards rightly deserves recognition and praise.

Benefits of setting standards

Where employees achieve high standards they improve the performance of the team, department and company which, in turn, leads to better profits, better job security and generally better morale among the staff. In other words, if you work in an environment where people work to high standards, you are more likely to end up working for a more financially secure company where people are generally happy at work.

Portfolio task 201.11   ➡ Links to LO2: assessment criterion 2.1

Produce a written summary which explains the purpose and benefits of agreeing and setting high standards for your work. Think about the standards which are expected of you at work. Why do you think these standards have been set? What do you think will be the result if you achieve/fail to achieve them?

Setting high standards for work

There are many ways in which you can set high standards for yourself at work such as:

- always aim to answer the phone within three rings
- always check your documents for spelling and accuracy
- maintain a professional approach to colleagues at all times
- complete your tasks on time or ahead of time.

When setting standards, it is important to make sure they are measurable. If a standard is not measurable, you will not be able to check accurately how well you are performing against it. Many businesses use SMART objectives to measure their performance. SMART stands for:

Specific — the objective relates to a particular task, such as answering the phone.

Measurable — the objective often involves a number, such as answering the phone within three rings.

Ambitious — an objective needs to be challenging or it will be too easy to achieve.

Realistic — it is important not to set unachievable objectives as this may demoralise staff.

Time-related — if you set a deadline by which you would like to have achieved the objective, this gives you a very clear time frame to work to.

How could you measure your progress towards achieving your goals?

> **Portfolio task 201.12** → Links to LO2: assessment criterion 2.2
>
> Write a short paragraph describing ways of setting high standards for your work. List three tasks that you carry out at work. For each one say how you could set yourself a higher standard of performance. Make sure the standards you set for yourself are realistic.

Taking on new challenges

Sometimes you will be presented with new challenges at work. These could involve having to learn new technologies, new skills or having to work with new people in another department. You will have the choice of whether to take on these new challenges, or whether to let them go to somebody else.

Why take on new challenges?

New challenges at work are good opportunities for you to develop your skills, add important experience to your CV and generally to try out new work activities and meet new colleagues.

All of these things could potentially lead to a new and better job and will help you to develop your future career within the company. There are many reasons for taking on new challenges, such as:

- to gain new experiences
- to develop new skills
- to try out new ways of working
- to test your abilities in different areas.

Benefits of new challenges

Taking on new challenges has many potential benefits for you and your career. These benefits include:

- a sense of achievement
- new experiences to be gained by doing something different
- learning new skills which will be good for future career opportunities
- working with new colleagues and developing good working relationships with them.

> **Portfolio task 201.13** → Links to LO2: assessment criterion 2.3
>
> Write a short report explaining the purpose and benefits of taking on new challenges at work. Remember to include examples of new challenges which you have been presented with in your job and discuss the benefits of these for you in your current position.

Adapting to change

Change happens all the time in business. As you go through your working life, you will see many changes in the way you have to work, in the way a business is run and in the products and services that it sells. With the fast pace of development in technology, in the future changes are likely to occur even more often, so the ability to adapt to change — and learn new ways of doing things — is going to be a key advantage to you.

Why adapt to change?

It is important to be able to adapt to change because:

● businesses are finding it necessary to make changes to survive

● these changes need positive people who will support new processes and learn new skills

● competition for jobs means people who are willing to adapt to change are better candidates and will be preferred over those who are not.

Benefits of being able to adapt to change

Being adaptable to change means you will be better able to embrace new ways of working and will be quick to learn new skills required of you. You will be more likely to benefit from changes in the workplace if you show that you can be adaptable and are not set in your ways. People who complain about new working practices and refuse to try to adapt to change are likely to be left behind with outdated skills. These people will find it difficult to remain in their jobs or find new ones.

There are several key benefits for those adaptable to change:

● you will learn new skills and technologies

● you are more likely to be successful in your job

● you are likely to be the best candidate for new positions in the company.

To help you appreciate the impact of changes which occur in business, take a look at the photos of the Microsoft® team in 1978 and as it is today.

Microsoft as it was in 1978, a small team of 11 people

Microsoft Corporation today, one of the world's largest businesses with more than 88,000 employees (June 2010, Microsoft website)

Many businesses have changed significantly since they were set up. How do you think you would manage change?

Activity 4

Make a list of some of the changes which have taken place in your company since you began working there. If there have not been any changes since you joined the company, ask your line manager or mentor about past changes and include these in your list. For each one, say whether you think they were positive or negative. Were there any problems associated with them? How were these problems handled? Use the table below to help you plan out your answer.

A version of this table, ready for you to complete, is available to download from www.contentextra.com/businessadmin

What change took place?	Positives and negatives	Problems associated with the change	How problems were handled

Portfolio task 201.14

→ Links to LO2: assessment criterion 2.4

Write a short report which explains the purpose and benefits of adapting to change. Remember to include the examples of changes that have taken place at the company where you work which you wrote about in Activity 4 and describe how you have had to adapt to them.

Functional Skills

English: Writing

You may be able to count your work from portfolio task 201.14 as evidence towards Level 2 Functional English: Writing.

Remember to check that you have used headings and correct spelling and grammar in your report and then print out the final corrected version.

Ask your assessor for guidance on checking that your work is as error free as possible.

Treating others with honesty, respect and consideration

In all areas of life, you should aim to treat the people with whom you come into contact with honesty, respect and consideration. This means showing regard for them and being thoughtful towards them and their feelings.

This is equally important in the workplace. Many businesses have signs and posters around their buildings stating that no abusive – rude or offensive – language or behaviour will be tolerated by employees of the company. This shows how important it is to employers that their staff are treated with respect.

Why treat others with honesty, respect and consideration?

The way in which people treat others at work is so important, simply because it says so much about their own personality. The way you behave – what you do – is as important, if not more so, than what you say.

If you work with someone who is always rude and impatient with you, it will be difficult for you to change your opinion of them. You may even try to avoid them in order not to be treated badly. If, on the other hand, you have a colleague who is consistently calm, patient and always makes time to help you when you need it, you will always go to this person as you can trust them to behave properly and to treat you with consideration.

The above examples highlight the key importance of behaviour at work. The reasons why we should always make a point of treating others properly are simple; everyone has the right to be treated fairly, and with consideration, in all areas of life including at work. Treating people unfairly may result in **allegations** of bullying, which is a serious offence and can result in **disciplinary action**.

Key terms

Allegation – an accusation against someone.

Disciplinary action – a set of procedures which a business will follow when taking action against staff if they fail to carry out their duties properly, or commit certain offences at work.

Key terms

Culture – the usual way in which things are done in a company and the general feeling of the workplace. A culture develops slowly over years and cannot be changed overnight.

Norm – the normal way in which things are done.

Staff retention – a measure of the number of people who leave a company each year. If staff retention is high, the company is retaining, or keeping, most of its staff; if it is low, many people are leaving.

For a link to *The Sunday Times* '100 Best Companies to Work For', please visit www.contentextra.com/businessadmin

Benefits of treating others with honesty, respect and consideration

There are many benefits of treating others with honesty, respect and consideration.

- When you treat others well, they are more likely to treat you well in return.
- You will gain a good reputation at work for treating others properly.
- It creates a **culture** at work where respectful behaviour is the **norm**.
- Staff will be happier to work for a company where they will always be treated properly.
- It creates a pleasant working environment for everyone, so employees are more likely to want to stay with the company. This means **staff retention** will be high.
- The company will be able attract the best candidates for jobs if it is known as a good place to work.

You can see from the list of benefits above that it is good for both employees and the company if staff treat each other well. Businesses with a reputation as a good place to work attract excellent publicity. For example, every year *The Sunday Times* publishes an annual list of the 100 best companies to work for. These companies will be able to attract the best employees.

✓ Checklist

Treating others well

Remember, treating others properly at work says a lot about you. Follow these steps to ensure you never let yourself down by your conduct towards others.

- Never send an email or make a phone call when you are angry – take five minutes to calm down. Only when you have looked again at the situation should you reply.

- If confronted by another colleague who is angry or upset, never get into a heated debate there and then. Instead, suggest a time later on to discuss the situation.

Portfolio task 201.15 → Links to LO2: assessment criterion 2.5

Write a short report which explains the purpose and benefits of treating others with honesty, respect and consideration. Think about this in relation to your job, and say why it is important to treat your colleagues with respect. Explain what you think might happen if you failed to do this.

Importance of behaviour in the workplace

A person's behaviour in the workplace is always important. In fact, the way you behave at work may determine your future success in your job. Behaviour includes what you do, what you say and the way you interact with others. You can choose to behave in a professional manner, which means you will give the best impression of yourself to colleagues. This means being professional in:

- what you say
- the way you say it
- how you act
- how you present yourself.

Activity 5

Complete the table below by listing three ways in which you can make sure you behave well at work.

Ways in which you can behave well at work	Benefit of this
1	
2	
3	

A version of this table, ready for you to complete, is available to download from www.contentextra.com/businessadmin

✓ Checklist

Behaving in a professional manner

Remember, others at work will make judgements about you based on your behaviour. If you are polite, hard working and well presented, others will see that you take pride in your job.

Follow these guidelines to make sure that you behave professionally at all times.

- Dress smartly – if you turn up to work looking scruffy, people will think that you do not care about your appearance or your job.

- Always be polite to people at work – if you are rude to others, they will think you are unable to deal with people properly, lack basic communication skills and you may not be considered for promotion.

Portfolio task 201.16   → Links to LO2: assessment criterion 2.6

Write a short paragraph which explains why your behaviour in the workplace is important. Use examples from your own job and give reasons to explain your answer.

Types of behaviour at work that show honesty, respect and consideration

In the last section, you looked at the importance of behaviour in the workplace. Now you will examine different types of behaviour at work and compare those that show honesty, respect and consideration with those that do not.

Activity 6

The table below includes some behaviours that show honesty, respect and consideration and some that do not. Read the behaviours in the left column and put 'Yes' or 'No' in the middle column remembering to give a reason for your answer.

Behaviour	Does this show honesty, respect and consideration? Y/N	Reason
Erin always makes time to listen to colleagues when they have problems.		
Sean regularly arrives late for work.		
Anne takes office stationery home for personal use.		
John always makes sure he drafts all his emails and re-reads them later before sending them.		
Shaheen, who runs the office, makes sure she speaks to each of her staff at least once a week to identify any problems.		
Jason often spends a long time watching YouTube videos at work.		

A version of this table, ready for you to complete, is available to download from www.contentextra.com/businessadmin

Portfolio task 201.17 → Links to LO2: assessment criterion 2.7

Write a short report describing types of behaviour at work that show honesty, respect and consideration and those that do not. It may be helpful to make a list of three of each type of behaviour and give reasons to explain your answer. You may want to use examples from the table you completed in Activity 6.

Evidence collection

In order for you to complete the remaining assessment criteria to pass this unit successfully, you will need to carry out various tasks at work and then produce evidence to show that you have demonstrated the required skills and competence.

Evidence can be collected in a number of different ways. For example, it can be either a signed witness testimony from a colleague or line manager, a copy of any related emails or letters you have produced, or a verbal discussion with your assessor.

Speak to your assessor to identify the best methods to use in order to complete each portfolio task and remember to keep copies of all the evidence which you produce.

Plan and be responsible for own work, supported by others

So far in this unit you have looked at some of the key issues which are important for you at work, such as:

- setting targets
- planning work
- problems which can occur at work
- working to deadlines and renegotiating timescales
- taking responsibility for your own work
- learning from mistakes.

All of these issues are central to you being effective in your job. Now that you have investigated what these issues mean, you will need to put them into practice by relating each of them directly to your job. The portfolio tasks which follow are practical in nature and require you to gather evidence of your competence in certain areas of your work.

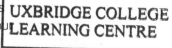

Portfolio task 201.18 → Links to LO3: assessment criteria 3.1, 3.2, 3.3 and 3.4

Gather evidence of your work to show your assessor that you have successfully carried out the four tasks outlined in the table below. Check with your assessor on the best ways of gathering evidence for each of the tasks before you begin.

Task	Evidence collected
1 Agree realistic targets and achievable timescales for own work.	
2 Plan work tasks to make best use of own time and available resources.	
3 Confirm effective working methods with others.	
4 Identify and report problems occurring in own work, using the support of other people when necessary.	

A version of this form, ready for you to complete, is available to download from www.contentextra.com/businessadmin

Portfolio task 201.19 → Links to LO3: assessment criteria 3.5, 3.6, 3.7 and 3.8

Gather evidence of your work to show your assessor that you have successfully carried out the four tasks outlined in the table below. Check with your assessor on the best ways of gathering evidence for each of the tasks before you begin.

Task	Evidence collected
1 Keep other people informed of progress.	
2 Complete work tasks to agreed deadlines or renegotiate timescales and plans in good time.	
3 Take responsibility for own work and accept responsibility for any mistakes made.	
4 Follow agreed work guidelines, procedures and, where needed, codes of practice.	

A version of this form, ready for you to complete, is available to download from www.contentextra.com/businessadmin

Behave in a way that supports effective working

Earlier in the unit you looked at the issue of behaviour in the workplace and why it is so important. Behaviour is the key yardstick by which you will be judged, both by your colleagues and your manager. In turn, the way in which you are judged will affect not only your current job but will also impact on your future development at the company. So, the better your behaviour, the better your prospects!

For the final part of this unit, you will focus on gathering evidence for your assessor to show how you have behaved in ways that support effective working.

Portfolio task 201.20   → Links to L04: assessment criteria 4.1, 4.2, 4.3, 4.4 and 4.5

Gather evidence of your work to show your assessor that you have successfully carried out the five tasks outlined in the table below. Check with your assessor on the best ways of gathering evidence for each of the tasks before you begin.

Task	Evidence collected
1 Set high standards for own work and show commitment to achieving these standards.	
2 Agree to take on new challenges if they arise.	
3 Adapt to new ways of working.	
4 Treat other people with honesty, respect and consideration.	
5 Help and support other people in work tasks.	

A version of this form, ready for you to complete, is available to download from www.contentextra.com/businessadmin

Check your knowledge

1 Why is it important to have guidelines and procedures at work?

a. To ensure everyone feels under pressure.

b. To ensure everyone follows the same methods to carry out certain activities.

c. To keep the boss happy.

d. It is illegal not to have them.

2 What is the main reason for planning your work?

a. To make sure you can leave early.

b. To ensure you make the most effective use of your time.

c. To reflect on your mistakes.

d. To keep yourself busy.

3 What does the term 'accountable' mean?

a. In trouble.

b. Financial.

c. Responsible.

d. Irresponsible.

4 What is a benefit of working to realistic targets at work?

a. The work will never be completed on time.

b. You can recognise all your mistakes.

c. It allows you to complete your tasks properly and to a good standard.

d. You will fall foul of legislation.

5 Why is it important to keep other people informed when work targets need to be changed?

a. It is none of their concern.

b. They need to know about changes as this may affect their other work and it allows them to make alternative arrangements if necessary.

c. So that they can do the work themselves.

d. They need to know about changes so that they can discuss them in meetings.

6 Why do you need to learn from mistakes?

a. To keep doing the same thing in future.

b. To make sure you do not make the same mistake again.

c. To get a pay rise.

d. To lower your performance.

7 What does it mean to 'reflect' on a situation?

a. To decide never to do it again.

b. To think back over an event and consider how you might do things differently next time.

c. To copy your behaviour.

d. To make future cost savings.

8 Why should you set yourself high standards at work?

a. Attaining high standards gives a tremendous sense of achievement.

b. My boss says I must.

c. Low standards mean I will lose my job.

d. High standards are impossible to achieve.

9 Why is your behaviour at work so important?

a. Behaviour at work does not really matter.

b. Behaviour is not part of the job description.

c. An individual's behaviour tells other people a lot about their personality and whether they are responsible or not.

d. Behaviour can be poor as long as no one gets injured.

10 Which of these types of behaviour shows honesty, respect and consideration?

a. Laughing behind someone's back.

b. Taking a sick day off work to go to a football match.

c. Listening to a colleague who has a problem and trying to suggest a solution.

d. Listening to music on your headphones while the boss is away at a meeting.

Answers to these questions can be found at www.contentextra.com/businessadmin

What your assessor is looking for

Each unit in this qualification comprises two types of assessment requirements. These are:

- knowledge-based learning outcomes
- performance indicators.

In order to prepare for and succeed in completing this unit, your assessor will require you to be able to demonstrate competence in all of the performance criteria listed in the table below.

Your assessor will guide you through the assessment process, but it is likely that for this unit you will need to:

- complete short written narratives or personal statements explaining your answers
- take part in professional discussions with your assessor to explain your answers verbally
- complete observations with your assessor ensuring that they can observe you carrying out your work tasks

- produce any relevant work products to help demonstrate how you have completed the assessment criteria
- ask your manager, a colleague or a customer for witness testimonies explaining how you have completed the assessment criteria.

The evidence which you generate for the assessment criteria in this unit may also count towards your evidence collection for some of the other units in this qualification. Your assessor will provide support and guidance on this.

The table below outlines the portfolio tasks which you need to complete for this unit, mapped to their associated assessment criteria.

Task and page reference	Mapping assessment criteria
Portfolio task 201.1 (page 5)	Assessment criterion: 1.1
Portfolio task 201.2 (page 6)	Assessment criterion: 1.2
Portfolio task 201.3 (page 7)	Assessment criterion: 1.3
Portfolio task 201.4 (page 9)	Assessment criterion: 1.4
Portfolio task 201.5 (page 10)	Assessment criterion: 1.5
Portfolio task 201.6 (page 13)	Assessment criterion: 1.6
Portfolio task 201.7 (page 15)	Assessment criterion: 1.7
Portfolio task 201.8 (page 16)	Assessment criterion: 1.8
Portfolio task 201.9 (page 17)	Assessment criterion: 1.9

Task and page reference	Mapping assessment criteria
Portfolio task 201.10 (page 18)	Assessment criterion: 1.10
Portfolio task 201.11 (page 19)	Assessment criterion: 2.1
Portfolio task 201.12 (page 20)	Assessment criterion: 2.2
Portfolio task 201.13 (page 20)	Assessment criterion: 2.3
Portfolio task 201.14 (page 22)	Assessment criterion: 2.4
Portfolio task 201.15 (page 25)	Assessment criterion: 2.5
Portfolio task 201.16 (page 26)	Assessment criterion: 2.6
Portfolio task 201.17 (page 27)	Assessment criterion: 2.7
Portfolio task 201.18 (page 28)	Assessment criteria: 3.1, 3.2, 3.3, 3.4
Portfolio task 201.19 (page 28)	Assessment criteria: 3.5, 3.6, 3.7, 3.8
Portfolio task 201.20 (page 29)	Assessment criteria: 4.1, 4.2, 4.3, 4.4, 4.5

Unit Q201 Manage own performance in a business environment

Unit Q202

Improve own performance in a business environment

What you will learn

- Understand how to improve own performance
- Be able to improve own performance using feedback
- Be able to agree own development needs using a learning plan

Introduction

In the workplace, it is important that you have the skills and ability to do a good job. How do you make sure that you are able to use and develop your skills to give you the competitive edge at work?

This unit will help you identify how to improve your own performance by using feedback from others. You will learn how to complete and review your personal learning plan to highlight your career opportunities as well as plan your learning and development needs.

This unit uses practical evidence from your workplace and links closely with Unit Q201 Manage own performance in a business environment. Now that you understand how performance and standard of work as well as behaviour affects others, you will need to consider how to improve your performance using feedback to learn and develop a career in business and administration.

How to improve own performance

Organisations aim to provide goods or services either to make a profit or give good value for money to the public. They rely on their employees to help them in this aim. Employers encourage their staff to learn and develop their skills to make sure that they are trained and skilled to do their jobs.

It is important to maintain standards for the work you produce and at the same time, develop other skills to meet new challenges and adapt to new ways of working.

Continuously improving performance

Purpose and benefits of improving performance for employees

As an employee, you need to understand why it is important for you to develop your skills continuously and know how this benefits you and your organisation.

Ask yourself what you would like to achieve from your job, what skills you have and what skills that you need to improve? Think of at least two ways that **continuous professional development (CPD)** can help you in the organisation.

Did you list any of the following reasons?

- Help you to progress in the organisation.
- Identify learning and development needs to fit in with the needs of the organisation.
- Enable you to develop other skills.
- Improve your existing abilities.
- Give you better opportunities in other organisations.

From this list, you will see that employees benefit from being skilled, experienced and qualified. They will be able to earn more, enjoy better chances for promotion and will be more competitive in the job market.

To be able to improve continuously, employees need to:

● know their strengths and areas for development

● be open to suggestions for improvement as this will show their employer that they want to learn and develop

● contribute to the organisation

● progress to more responsible jobs.

Discussions and feedback therefore become an important part of daily work life.

Purpose and benefits of improving performance for organisations

Do you think it is important for employers to enable their employees to continuously learn and develop their skills and abilities? Before reading on, think of at least two reasons why it would benefit businesses to do this.

Where employees continuously improve their performance, an organisation will be able to:

● meet its aims in a cost-effective and efficient way

● provide more effective customer service

● fill any existing skills gaps

● plan for future growth or development.

For a business to provide appropriate services and/or goods to customers, it needs to have skilled, qualified and able employees.

Skills audit

An employer or the human resources department may conduct a **skills audit** to identify the existing skills, qualifications and abilities of their staff. By planning in advance, the business will be able to identify any gaps in the workforce. For example, if a new photocopier is introduced with scanning and faxing facilities, the staff using it will need to be identified and training provided. The skills audit will show who should undergo training before installation so that they will be able to use the equipment efficiently and maybe even train other employees.

A skills audit will also enable businesses to plan for expansion or contraction, recruit new appropriately qualified employees, train existing ones to fill any skills gap, continue to provide their existing service or product or even expand the range of products and services they offer. The skills audit can even be used as a planning tool to train future managers.

If employees are encouraged to improve their performance at work, they will be motivated to do better in order to progress in the organisation. It will also enable the organisation to retain its staff who, through their experience and knowledge of the business, will help to improve quality and standards to customers.

> **Key term**
>
> **Skills audit** – the process of measuring existing staff's qualifications and skills against the skills, knowledge and experience required for the future.

Being able to receive and act on feedback will help you to develop your skills

Encouraging and accepting feedback from others

In most organisations, you will be able to learn and develop using feedback from your supervisor, colleagues or even customers.

When working in any office environment, you will need to record, process or send information. In order to be able to do this well, it is important to have good written and verbal communication skills so that you can pass on messages and information accurately and in a timely way. By developing and constantly improving your skills, you will have better career opportunities because you will be able to do your job more effectively.

Purpose and benefits of encouraging feedback for employees

By encouraging feedback from your supervisor, team members or colleagues, you will be able to learn from their experience and knowledge. Through talking to them and observing how they work, you will improve your skills, for example how to deal politely with complaints. Understanding your role will also help you to identify job opportunities and positions either in the organisation or other businesses.

Feedback may be about recognising achievements, identifying mistakes or highlighting skills that need to be improved or developed. Being able to use feedback, without taking it personally, will help you improve your performance and enable you to develop your existing skills and abilities. Keeping an open mind and reacting positively at work shows that you are a professional and willing to keep learning to do better.

Purpose and benefits of encouraging feedback for organisations

Organisations that encourage feedback and open discussion among employees will benefit from continuous improvement, which will enable them to provide better service and quality as well as new product development for future expansion or growth.

For the organisation to benefit from employees who want to continuously learn and develop themselves, feedback to employees has to be given positively, and not taken personally. The **appraisal system**, which provides an opportunity for open discussion between the supervisor or manager and employee, is commonly used by businesses to provide feedback. Other methods include informal discussions or on-the-spot feedback when work is being given or completed.

Purpose and benefits of accepting feedback for employees

Feedback helps to identify what you are doing well and where you need to improve. It is important to identify areas for improvement as this will help you work more effectively and provide a better service to customers and colleagues. Acting on feedback helps you become a better employee, and may help you to gain a promotion.

Key term

Appraisal system – one-to-one discussions that are held privately between a supervisor or manager and individual staff to review progress, performance and responsibilities. The process may take place annually or twice a year and gives employees the chance to talk about their achievements and identify areas that they want to develop. Appraisal should be a two-way process where information is shared and plans made for the employee's future development.

✓ Checklist
Receiving feedback

When receiving feedback, you need to:

- listen
- keep an open mind
- have a positive attitude, e.g. sit straight, make eye contact to show you are paying attention
- ask questions if you are not sure
- make notes of comments.

Remember that it is about your work, not you as a person, so do not take feedback personally.

Table 202.1 summarises the purpose and methods of feedback and identifies the people who are able to provide you with feedback on your performance.

Purpose	Methods	People who can give you feedback
Learn from mistakes Review progress on tasks Recognise achievements Identify strength and areas for development Help set targets for development	Through formal appraisal system Informal one-to-one discussion Peer assessment Self-evaluation Observation	Supervisor/Line Manager Colleagues or peers Customers

Table 202.1: *Purpose and methods of feedback*

Purpose and benefits of accepting feedback for organisations

By encouraging feedback among employees, an organisation will be able to:

● improve quality and standard of work on a daily basis
● retain experienced and skilled staff
● identify its employees' training and development needs
● use employees' skills and knowledge effectively and efficiently
● plan in advance for recruitment
● plan and budget for training to meet future expansion or contraction.

Identifying management or leadership potential in employees through formal appraisals enables organisations to plan for the future. This is known as **succession planning** — employees may be trained for several years to prepare them for management positions.

Key term

Succession planning – process of identifying internal staff to prepare and develop them for more responsible senior jobs/positions.

Portfolio task 202.1

→ Links to LO1: assessment criteria 1.1 and 1.2

1 Complete the table below to provide evidence of your knowledge and understanding of the purpose and benefits of improving own performance in an organisation for both employees and the organisation itself.

Purpose and benefits of continuously improving performance at work	
For employee	For organisation

2 Produce either a poster or brochure with appropriate headings to show your understanding of the purpose and benefits of encouraging and accepting feedback from others to the employees and the organisation.

Functional skills

English: Speaking, listening and communication

When you discuss your answers with your peers, you may be able to count it as evidence towards Level 1 Functional English: Speaking, listening and communication through taking part in an informal discussion.

To give you some ideas, there are suggested headings for your poster or brochure on www.contentextra. com/businessadmin

How learning and development can improve own work, benefit organisations and identify career options

Your role in the business is important as each individual plays a part in making the organisation a success. Professionalism, responsibility and commitment to providing good, if not excellent, customer service means the business will have a better chance of surviving in any economic situation.

Purpose of learning and development and its benefits to organisations

Technology and working practices change rapidly. Continuous learning and regular training will help you to keep on top of developments in the workplace and will help you and your organisation to remain competitive.

Identifying learning and development needs will give employees a starting point to:

- update skills to meet demand for jobs and changes
- update knowledge due to changes in policies, regulations, and so on
- develop new skills to meet changing demand and trends in technology
- gain new accredited qualifications to progress in their career
- improve team working skills
- develop appropriate habits or behaviour.

As shown in Table 202.1 above, the different methods for receiving feedback may be through the formal appraisal system, informal discussion, self-evaluation, observation, peer assessment or one-to-one reviews when tasks are being distributed or returned. Regular feedback may be used to review employees' progress to keep track of any improvement or achievements. Annual reviews are used to identify specific training or learning needs that may have been highlighted over a period of time. Meeting employees' learning needs will improve their knowledge and understanding while helping them to develop the skills required to do their current jobs better or learn new skills for new responsibilities. This is essential to keep employees motivated and aware of their role in the organisation.

Benefits for the organisation may include reduced cost of training and recruitment, and for employees, the chance for internal promotion. The skills and knowledge acquired by employees will give a sense of continuity and better staff morale. This will help businesses retain existing customers who may recommend new ones as they are confident when dealing with the organisation.

Portfolio task 202.2

→ Links to LO1: assessment criterion 1.3

Complete the table below to provide evidence of your knowledge and understanding of how learning and development can improve own work and benefit the organisation.

Purpose and benefits of learning and development	
How learning and development can improve own work as an employee	Benefits to organisation

Functional skills

English: Develop, present and communicate information

When you are learning to summarise information you will be developing your skills to prepare for the English Functional Skills exam at Level 1 or 2.

A version of this table, ready for you to complete, is available to download from www.contentextra.com/businessadmin

Career options within organisations

In this section, you will look at how learning and development can improve your work and identify career options for you as an administrator. You will then be able to explain how suitably skilled and qualified administrators will benefit organisations. From your research, you will be able to describe the possible career progression routes in business administration together with possible development opportunities for yourself.

The administrator in a business provides support and helps others to do their jobs more efficiently and effectively. Often the administrator is competent in using IT software packages and has excellent communication skills.

CfA – Business skills @ work is a government-recognised body that sets the standards for business skills in the UK. In research carried out in 2008, the CfA identified the following skills that administrators need in order to do their job:

- IT skills
- managing information
- planning and organising
- communication
- problem solving
- people management.

These skills will be developed over time as you gain experience and knowledge from employment and/or training. Some skills can be learned through studying, observation and asking questions while others can only be improved through hard work and practice. The skills listed by the CfA are **transferable**, which means they are equally important in a wide variety of jobs and organisations. For example, to learn how to use word-processing software well you need to practise using it so that you become familiar with its features and functions. Once you know the main functions and have touch-typing skills, you will be able to produce professional documents quickly and accurately which will be attractive skills for a wide range of employers. Your skills at this level will also include the ability to listen and follow instructions accurately.

As you progress to higher levels of responsibility, you will learn to use different operating systems and be able to manage information more effectively for different purposes. This may include learning how to solve problems and analyse information for decision making. You may even be supervising other members of staff.

This example shows how basic IT skills can be developed to provide you with a career path in managing information and decision making. It also requires you to plan and organise your time and other resources, communicate with others and manage staff to ensure that you meet deadlines and produce professional, accurate work. This may relate to any sector or organisation and depends on the job role and the level of responsibility.

> **Key term**
>
> **Transferable skills** – special skills, such as problem solving, which are useful in all jobs.

Unit Q202 Improve own performance in a business environment

Possible career progression routes

Further research by the CfA shows that the largest skills gaps exist in customer handling, written and verbal communication skills and problem solving as well as office skills and technical competency (see Figure 202.1). In 2007, 30 per cent of companies had trouble recruiting qualified administration staff compared to 25 per cent in 2006.

Looking at skills gaps can help you to identify the skills that you might want to develop. As you progress in your career, you will be learning how to manage people, plan and organise your resources more efficiently and effectively while managing information to achieve your goals. Use the list in Figure 202.1 to identify the area or skills you are interested in developing, either in your present organisation or future career. To consider the career options available to you, you will need to think about the kind of job you are doing and your potential for development.

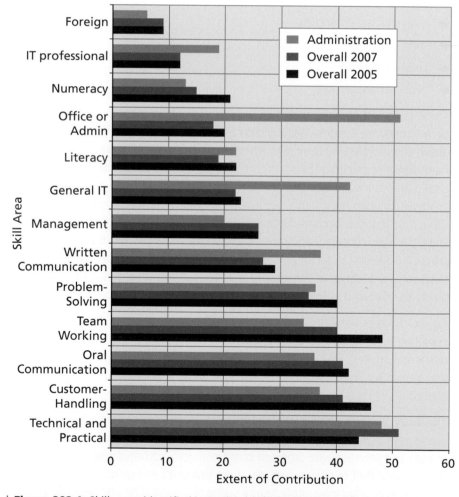

Figure 202.1: *Skills gaps identified in England (CfA (2008)* Gap Analysis: Business Administration and Governance Skills Market, *p. 20; cfa.uk.com)*

Figure 202.2 shows the suggested career option at each stage with the different levels of both vocational and academic qualifications, depending on your ability and preference. Vocational qualifications are achieved through study and practical application of knowledge like your NVQ. Academic qualifications are normally based on knowledge building, that is, studying for a degree. The administrative knowledge and experience you gain will be transferable and you will be able to work in almost any sector. To benefit from this career, you need to look for opportunities to develop yourself continuously through distance learning, courses, work shadowing, and so on. After a couple of years, you might decide to specialise in a particular area or function such as legal or finance.

Table 202.2 shows some of the specialist areas and knowledge required in various sectors.

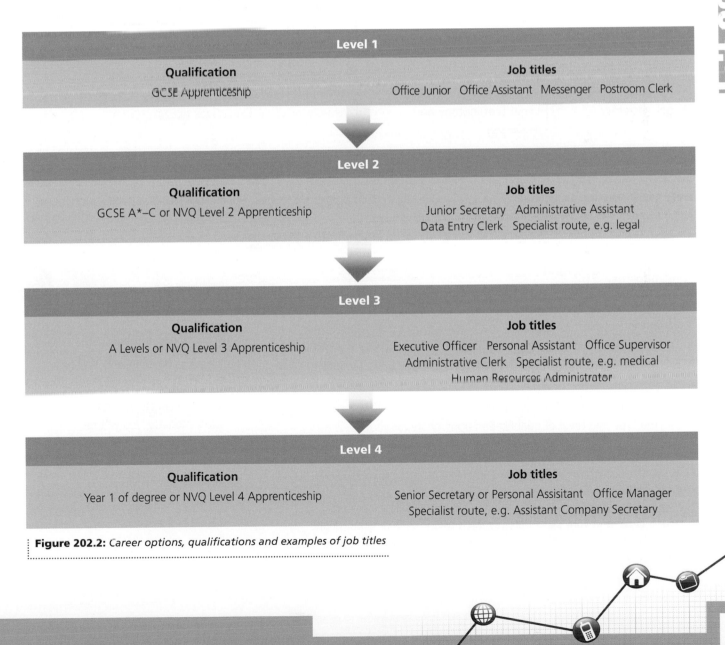

Figure 202.2: *Career options, qualifications and examples of job titles*

Specialist roles	Specialist knowledge required	Professional body
HR administrator	Human resources knowledge, such as recruitment legislation and data protection	Chartered Institute of Personnel and Development (CIPD)
Sales/marketing administrator	Marketing knowledge	Chartered Institute of Marketing (CIM)
Property administrator	Legislation knowledge	Institute of Professional Administrators (IPA) or Institute of Chartered Secretaries and Administrators (ICSA)
Finance administrator	Knowledge of finance	
Registrar	Knowledge of finance	Institute of Administrative Management (IAM)
Medical secretary	Medical terminology	Institute of Professional Administrators (IPA) or Association of Medical Secretaries, Practice Managers, Administrators and Receptionists (AMSPAR)
Legal secretary	Legal terminology and processes	Institute of Legal Executives (ILEX)
School secretary	Legislation relating to children	Institute of Administrative Management (IAM)

Table 202.2: *Specialist administrator roles, knowledge required and professional bodies (Source: CfA (2008)* Gap Analysis: Business Administration and Governance Skills Market, *p. 23; cfa.uk.com)*

Portfolio task 202.3

→ Links to LO1: assessment criteria 1.3 and 1.4

1 Carry out research on the different specialist roles you are interested in, using the relevant professional and training provider websites. The suggested professional bodies are given in Table 202.2 and you will be able to obtain job profiles and qualifications required for the relevant jobs. This will form part of your evidence for this task.

From your research, find out the following:
- the type and level of qualification appropriate for you
- the type of organisation you would like to work for
- a specialist area available as a career option.

You may need to conduct primary and secondary research. For example, your primary source may be an interview with a practice manager in an NHS clinic and your secondary research might be finding out about qualifications and training provided in your area. Add a bibliography to show evidence of your research.

Functional skills

English: Reading and Writing

If you are able to summarise your research effectively and professionally, you will be preparing yourself for the Reading and Writing Level 1 Functional Skills English exam.

2 Use a chart to describe the possible career progression routes for you. An example is shown below:

Where am I now?	Where I want to be in two years' time?	Where I want to be in five years' time?
I am currently working as an Administrative Assistant in a private clinic. My responsibilities are …	I want to pursue a career in Office or Medical Administration, I have checked the website for AMSPAR and found that …	I wish to become a Practice Manager in a private or NHS Clinic. The Practice Manager is responsible for …

Possible development opportunities

To help employees learn more about the business, organisations might suggest work shadowing or coaching to provide promotional opportunities. In other situations, employees might take part in job rotation or job enlargement which enables staff to learn more about the business while improving and developing new skills. Here are examples of both internal and external training methods:

A version of this chart, ready for you to complete, is available to download from www.contentextra.com/businessadmin

- day release
- job enlargement
- course-specific seminar
- job rotation
- networking
- on-the-job training
- distance learning
- coaching
- short course
- work shadowing
- online training or e-learning.

Training can help you to learn more about your role or company, or help you develop your skills

Unit Q202

Improve own performance in a business environment

Activity

This activity will help you to identify what you could develop. Think of a situation where you had to use your skills, knowledge and attributes. For example, when you dealt with a member of staff or customer, how did you speak to them and what type of information did you have to give them? If possible, compare skills with a colleague or friend.

Use the list from Table 202.3 to help you identify the skills that you possess and/or areas that you need to develop. You might be able to add a few more yourself.

Knowledge	Skills	Attributes
• Systems and procedures to help you do your job • Role of all employees in organisation • Structure of organisation • Business purpose and code of practice	• Good verbal communication when dealing with all customers • Able to listen and understand customers' needs • Able to follow instructions and complete tasks in good time and accurately • Good written communication when dealing with all customers	• Punctuality • Observe confidentiality • Honesty • Courtesy

Table 202.3: *Examples of skills, attributes and knowledge required by administrators*

You will have found that knowledge, skills and attributes are all equally important depending on the context, such as the type of organisation, situation and your customers' needs.

Improve own performance using feedback

For this learning outcome you will need to show how you used feedback to improve your own performance. This is a practical section which requires you to think about your recent experience when you completed tasks at work and appropriate feedback for improving your performance.

When feedback is being given by your supervisor or colleagues, do not take things personally. Feedback is aimed at helping you to improve your skills and/or knowledge, not about you as a person. You need to see feedback as useful for your development which is why it is often referred to as **constructive feedback**.

Key term

Constructive feedback – feedback given to staff based on achievements or areas for improvement. It may not always be about negative issues and is intended to be honest feedback without being personal. To be constructive, feedback must be timely and provide solutions to help someone improve.

Portfolio task 202.4

→ Links to LO2: assessment criteria 2.1, 2.2 and 2.3

Use a log sheet like the one shown below to help you complete the following tasks.

1 Think of at least *three* instances when you have encouraged feedback from others and what happened afterwards. Write them down in the log sheet.

2 Use at least *two* of these feedback sessions and make sure your supervisor signs off your work and the log sheet to confirm the feedback agreed.

3 Show evidence of work completed from the feedback or a witness statement from your supervisor.

Functional skills

English: Speaking, listening and communication

In discussing your performance with your assessor, you may be able to count it as evidence towards Level 1 Functional English: Speaking, listening and communication as you are taking part in an informal discussion.

Log sheet for work completed from _____ **to** _____

Date	Type of work or task given	Feedback from supervisor	Completed task (signed off)

A version of this log sheet, ready for you to complete, is available to download from www.contentextra.com/businessadmin

Improve own performance in a business environment **Unit Q202**

Office life

Linda's story

My name is Linda Scott. I'm 19 and started working for RA Insurance Brokers three months ago. Since joining, I've learned lots of terms used in the insurance business and the different types of documents required. My day is mostly spent typing documents for all the staff.

Ask the expert

Q Yesterday, my supervisor asked me to complete a computer spreadsheet. It had lots of complicated figures and she told me to use the calculations facility in Excel. I wasn't sure what she meant or where to start. I really struggled with the task and it took me the whole day to complete. This morning she called me into her office to give me feedback on my work. She said that the spreadsheet contained lots of mistakes. I was really upset because I'd put so much effort into the task. What should I have done?

A When your supervisor gave you the task, you should have explained that you weren't familiar with Excel and needed help. Either your supervisor could have helped you or she could have asked another member of staff to do so. In future, as insurance work deals with calculations and probabilities, you could identify this as a development need. For example, you could start by asking colleagues who have more experience, observe how others prepare similar tasks or ask for samples or templates. You could also develop your knowledge by referring to simple instructions manuals, use 'How to' books, or the Help function in Excel to learn how to use it more efficiently. Remember, do not take criticisms personally as it is not about you but how you could improve your work.

Top tips

- Use eye contact to show that you are listening and nod to show you understand what is being said.
- Ask questions if you are not sure how to carry out your work.
- Request for feedback on all work that you complete so that you can improve your work.
- Observe how others complete their work and learn from them.
- If you do not agree, give your opinions calmly, but do not take things personally.
- Keep a daily diary of what you do. You will be surprised at how much you have learned over time.
- From your diary, you will be able to identify at least three possible development opportunities that you might be able to implement each year.

Agree own development needs using a learning plan

Now that you have identified your future plans, you will be able to complete your learning plan. To enable you to develop consistently throughout your career, you may find it helpful to keep a diary or log of your daily tasks or responsibilities. This will act as a reference for identifying your training needs, achievements and provide feedback on your progress during your appraisals. If you do not write down your experiences, you are likely to forget them as time goes by and it will take you longer to think about what you have learned and what you already know.

If you use the diary or log effectively to review your progress, you will show that you are keen to learn and this will develop your confidence. It will also help you to keep track of your progress and achievements for your annual appraisal with your supervisor.

To complete this learning outcome, you will complete a practical task to show how learning and development can help you progress in your career.

Key terms

Job description – an outline of the job title, aims of the job, name of supervisor and duties, usually written by the employee's manager. An example is shown in Figure 202.3.

Person specification – lists the types of qualification, skills and qualities of the person for the job, usually written by the employee's manager. An example is shown in Figure 202.4.

Unit Q202

Portfolio task 202.5
→ Links to LO1: assessment criterion 1.5 (task 2); LO2: assessment criterion 3.1 (task 1)

Use presentation software to design attractive and relevant slides to give the following information.

1 *Your research.* Summarise the skills and knowledge you need to do your job using your **job description** and **person specification** which was given to you by your manager or is available from the human resources department. If this is not available, look for one on the Internet, similar to the job role that you currently have. From portfolio task 202.3, suggest possible development opportunities that you can achieve in the next two years. Then, identify how these development opportunities can improve your performance.

2 *The presentation.* Using at least three slides, summarise the above information in a presentation using appropriate headings and images to make it interesting. You could use the following headings to structure your presentation:

- My current skills and knowledge
- My ambition and 5-year plan
- My development needs.

Functional skills

English: Develop, present and communicate information

If you are able to summarise your research and give a professional presentation, you will be able to meet the requirements for an effective presentation at Level 2.

Improve own performance in a business environment

JOB DESCRIPTION

Department: Support Services

Job title: Administrative Assistant

Hours of work: 37.5 hours per week; 9am to 5.30pm Monday to Friday

Salary scale: £12,000 – £15,000

Reporting to: Contracts Manager

Job purpose: To provide administrative support to the team.
To handle customer enquiries by phone, post and online.
To prepare all necessary documents relating to contracts, suppliers and sales.

Responsibilities:

1. Answer the telephone and pass on messages.

2. Welcome and deal with visitors.

3. Word process and produce documents.

4. Maintain effective customer relations with staff and other customers.

5. File and manage customer records.

6. Organise team meetings.

7. Handle outgoing and internal mail and correspondence.

8. Use office equipment such as printer, fax and photocopier safely and effectively.

9. Attend any training courses or team events as requested by the Contracts Manager.

10. Maintain staff confidentiality at all times.

11. Undertake any other relevant duties identified by the Contracts Manager.

Figure 202.3: *A sample job description*

PERSON SPECIFICATION

Department: Support Services

Job title: Administrative Assistant

Scale: 1/2

QUALIFICATIONS/EXPERIENCE	ESSENTIAL	DESIRABLE
GCSE level or equivalent including GCSE English at Grade C or above	X	
NVQ/SNVQ Level 2 Business Administration		X
L2 Certificate in Text Processing		X

Skills and attributes

1. Ability to work with people across a wide range of levels and responsibilities.
2. Ability to communicate well with all customers.
3. Ability to work in a team.
4. Ability to write messages, prepare routine letters and simple reports with appropriate structure and accuracy.
5. Attention to detail.
6. Good keyboarding skills.
7. Trustworthy and reliable.
8. Ability to maintain confidentiality.
9. Flexible and able to prioritise workload on a daily basis.
10. Self-motivated to learn and develop the necessary skills.
11. Proficient in using a computer (especially Word, Excel and MS Office).

Figure 202.4: *A sample person specification for a job*

Portfolio task 202.6

→ Links to LO3: assessment criteria 3.2, 3.3, 3.4

When you have completed the presentation for portfolio task 202.5, add the information into your learning plan. A sample of a learning plan is shown below.

JOB SKILLS AND KNOWLEDGE			
Skills and/or knowledge to be developed	Learning and development method	When	Feedback after event
Telephone skills	Coaching and observation	30 March 2010	I made notes as I observed Katie handling the calls with internal and external customers.
PERSONAL DEVELOPMENT			
Area or skills for development	Learning and development method	When	Feedback after event
Assertiveness	In-house event	12 Aug 2010	

A template of the learning plan, ready for you to complete, is available to download from www.contentextra.com/businessadmin

Check your knowledge

1 What does the M in SMART targets stand for?

a. Meaningful.

b. Method.

c. Measurable.

d. Message.

2 Which methods could develop your skills without going on a training course?

a. Seminar.

b. Job enlargement.

c. Job enrichment.

d. Day release.

3 Which of the following is *not* a benefit of receiving feedback?

a. You are able to learn from your mistakes.

b. It helps you improve your skills.

c. It gives you a chance to get to know your team.

d. It identifies your achievements or strengths.

4 Which of these statements is a SMART target?

a. I will never be absent from work.

b. I will improve my attendance at work to 95% by December 2011.

c. I will make sure I complete my work every day.

d. I will be punctual for work this week.

5 What type of feedback helps you to improve your skills through discussion with your supervisor?

a. Competent.

b. Constructive.

c. Capable.

d. Critical.

6 Which of following will *not* help you when encouraging and receiving feedback?

a. Listen and make notes of any feedback.

b. Ask questions if you are not sure of the comments.

c. Keep calm if you are not happy with the comments.

d. Avoid eye contact.

7 Which document lists the skills, qualifications and qualities of the person who will be doing a particular job?

a. Job description.

b. Skills audit.

c. Person specification.

d. Succession plan.

8 Name the process of identifying internal staff by preparing and developing them for a more responsible senior position.

a. Job description.

b. Skills audit.

c. Person specification.

d. Succession plan.

9 What is the name of a document that provides the title of a job, name of supervisor as well as list of duties and responsibilities?

a. Job description.

b. Skills audit.

c. Person specification.

d. Succession plan.

10 What is the name of the process of measuring employees' skills and competencies for meeting future needs?

a. Job description.

b. Skills audit.

c. Person specification.

d. Succession plan.

Answers to these questions can be found at www.contentextra.com/businessadmin

What your assessor is looking for

Each unit in this qualification comprises two types of assessment requirements. These are:

- knowledge-based learning outcomes
- performance indicators.

In order to prepare for and succeed in completing this unit, your assessor will require you to be able to demonstrate competence in all of the performance criteria listed in the table below.

Your assessor will guide you through the assessment process, but it is likely that for this unit you will need to:

- complete short written narratives or personal statements explaining your answers
- take part in professional discussions with your assessor to explain your answers verbally

- complete observations with your assessor ensuring that they can observe you carrying out your work tasks
- produce any relevant work products to help demonstrate how you have completed the assessment criteria
- ask your manager, a colleague or a customer for witness testimonies explaining how you have completed the assessment criteria.

The evidence which you generate for the assessment criteria in this unit may also count towards your evidence collection for some of the other units in this qualification. Your assessor will provide support and guidance on this.

The table below outlines the portfolio tasks which you need to complete for this unit, mapped to their associated assessment criteria.

Task and page reference	Mapping assessment criteria
Portfolio task 202.1 (page 39)	Assessment criteria: 1.1, 1.2
Portfolio task 202.2 (page 40)	Assessment criterion: 1.3
Portfolio task 202.3 (pages 44–45)	Assessment criteria: 1.3, 1.4
Portfolio task 202.4 (page 47)	Assessment criteria: 2.1, 2.2, 2.3
Portfolio task 202.5 (page 49)	Assessment criteria: 1.5 (task 2), 3.1 (task 1)
Portfolio task 202.6 (page 52)	Assessment criteria: 3.2, 3.3, 3.4

Unit Q203

Work in a business environment

What you will learn

- Understand how to respect other people at work
- Understand how to maintain security and confidentiality at work and deal with concerns
- Understand the purpose and procedures for keeping waste to a minimum in a business environment
- Understand procedures for disposal of hazardous materials
- Know how to support sustainability in an organisation
- Be able to respect and support other people at work in an organisation
- Be able to maintain security and confidentiality
- Be able to support sustainability and minimise waste in an organisation

Introduction

In this unit, you will explore some of the key issues which you are likely to experience when working in a business environment.

Respect and the importance of respecting others at work is the starting point for establishing good, professional working relationships with colleagues. This unit looks at the ways in which you can respect other people who may be from different age groups, social classes or ethnic backgrounds and have varying personality types.

Security and confidentiality at work are also important issues and you will investigate the way in which you can maintain the security and confidentiality of sensitive and personal data and how to deal with concerns about this from others at work.

Nowadays, a priority for most businesses is to minimise waste, and you will look at how this can be achieved in your company. Hazardous materials must be disposed of correctly and you will learn about the procedures for doing this safely.

Finally, you will investigate what sustainability means for businesses and look at ways in which you can support sustainability at work. This issue is very important as it goes further than your own company and affects us all.

No matter what your line of business, issues such as respect, security and sustainability are fundamental to all of us, in every aspect of our lives. Learning about them will provide you with valuable knowledge and insight which will benefit you throughout your career.

How to respect other people at work

In employment terms, diversity usually refers to differences in gender, age, ethnic origin, sexual orientation and ability or disability. It is important to have a good understanding of the nature of diversity at work and how this impacts on all employees, because this will help you to respect the differences in people's abilities, backgrounds, values, customs and beliefs, enabling you to treat them in a way that takes account of their needs. Learning from others at work will also help you to develop your own skills and abilities.

Diversity

Diversity is something which we should all celebrate. The diversity everywhere in our lives is precisely what makes it so rich and varied. Quite simply, diversity means difference. It refers to differences in terms of age, gender, role, background, skill level, skill type, beliefs, customs and traditions. Diversity also includes differences in terms of sexual orientation (whether a person is heterosexual, homosexual or bisexual) and ability or disability.

How does a diverse workforce benefit an organisation?

Think about your job and the organisation you work for. How many people work there? Of these people, how many different age groups are there? How many different ethnic backgrounds are there? How many different skill levels and types are there? Depending upon the size, location and nature of your company, there could potentially be vast numbers of different types of people. All of these different types of people bring with them different experiences and abilities which add huge value to the business. We will look at this value in a little more detail in the next section.

Respecting diversity

Most medium and large businesses publicly declare their commitment to respecting diversity in the workforce in their equal opportunity or diversity policies. For example, Tesco is proud of its diversity and:

> '... strives to provide an inclusive environment where all difference is valued, people are able to be themselves, enjoy coming to work and realise their full potential, regardless of their gender, marital status, race, age, sexual orientation, creed, ethnic origin, religion or belief, or disability.'

Source: www.tescoplc.com

The retailer also has a large number of initiatives in place to underpin the company's commitment to diversity. For example:

- it works with disability employment agencies, Remploy and the Shaw Trust, in order to actively increase the number of disabled people who work for it
- Tesco Women's Network aims to help female managers and directors progress – 'We want women to do as well as men at Tesco.'

Key term

Discrimination – when someone is treated unfairly on the basis of their ethnic origin, religion, age, sexual orientation, gender or ability.

- 'Out at Tesco', launched in 2009, is a network for lesbian, gay, bisexual and transgender (LGBT) staff in the UK. Its aim is to encourage and support LGBT staff to feel comfortable and happy at work and to network with others who join the initiative

- over the last 20 years, Tesco has been running campaigns to attract and recruit older staff (Source: www.tescoplc.com).

Legislation

Employers must ensure that they stay within the law when they employ staff. In the UK, employment legislation is in place to protect employees from **discrimination** on the basis of:

- gender
- sexual orientation
- age
- ethnic background, beliefs and creed
- disability.

This means that employees have the right not to be discriminated against on the basis of any of the above factors. They can also take an employer to an employment tribunal if they believe that they have been unfairly treated at work.

The latest piece of legislation to come into effect is the Equality Act 2010, which will replace previous legislation.

Activity 1

To find out more about employment legislation and what it means in practice, as well as the 2010 Equality Act, take a look at the website of the Employment and Human Rights Commission. For a link to the website, please visit www.contentextra.com/businessadmin

Portfolio task 203.1

→ Links to L01: assessment criterion 1.1

1   Write a short paragraph which describes what is meant by diversity and say why you think it should be valued.

2   Find any relevant diversity policies or guidelines from your company and see what they say. Use the information from these documents to help you write your answer. Remember to keep copies of these documents for your portfolio of evidence. If there are no relevant documents available, search the Chartered Institute of Personnel and Development website which contains useful information on diversity. For a link to the CIPD website, please visit www.contentextra.com/businessadmin

Functional skills

English: Speaking, listening and communication

If you are asked to take part in a professional discussion with your assessor for portfolio task 203.1, you may be able to count this as evidence towards Functional English Level 2: Speaking, listening and communication. You will need to prepare for this discussion by reading over your work for the task and making sure that you are fully prepared to give explanations of the key points, as well as answering any questions which you may be asked.

Treating other people with sensitivity

Traditionally, equal opportunity and anti-discrimination legislation, along with company policies, treated all groups of protected employees as homogenous, that is, they were all treated the same. However, it is now understood that people at work need to be treated in a way that is tailored to their individual needs. A one-size-fits-all approach is no longer acceptable.

✓ Checklist

Dealing with staff

When dealing with other members of staff with disabilities, think about the person and not the disability. Speak to them in the same way that you would to an able-bodied colleague.

Portfolio task 203.2   → Links to LO1: assessment criterion 1.2

Write a short paragraph which describes how to treat other people in a way that is sensitive to their needs. Give examples of how you have done this at work.

Respecting others' abilities, background, values, customs and beliefs

In order to be able to treat people in a way that respects their abilities, background, values, customs and beliefs, you will need to have an open mind. Talking to and mixing with people from other walks of life, creeds, nationalities, age groups and abilities will not only broaden your own horizons but you will also benefit from learning about other people's experiences.

✓ Checklist

Business policies and practices

Remember, the UK is a multi-cultural society and business policies and practices must take this into account in their treatment of staff.

Religions in Britain

Another important aspect to consider in the treatment of others is that they may have important customs and religious activities which must be observed at certain times of the year. You do not have to become an expert, but if you know a little about these, it will go a long way to making them feel valued and respected at work. Figure 203.1 shows the major religions practised in Britain.

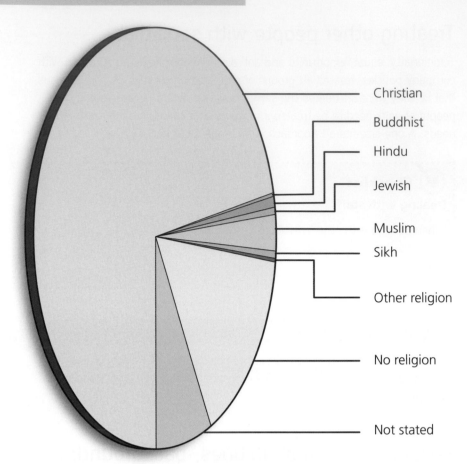

Source: Census, April 2001, Office for National Statistics.

Diversiton produces a 'diversity calendar' that lists dates for the main feasts, festivals and holy days observed by Islam, Buddhism, Christianity, Hunduism, Bahá'í faith, Judaism, Sikhism, Confucianism, Zoroastrianism. It also includes secular dates. For a link to the website, see www.contentextra.com/businessadmin

Religion	Thousands	%
Christian	41,015	71.8
Buddhist	149	0.3
Hindu	558	1.0
Jewish	267	0.5
Muslim	1,589	2.8
Sikh	336	0.6
Other religion	159	0.3
No religion	8,596	15.1
Not stated	4,434	7.8
Total	57,104	100

Figure 203.1: *The population of Great Britain by religion, April 2001 (Source: Office for National Statistics*

Note: Totals may not add due to rounding.

Portfolio task 203.3 ➡ Links to LO1: assessment criterion 1.3

Produce a short report which describes how to treat other people in a way that respects their abilities, background, values, customs and beliefs. Try to include an example of how you have done this in your job, or how you would go about it if you have not yet had the opportunity to do so.

Learning from others at work

As mentioned earlier, Tesco has been running campaigns for years in order to attract older workers to their company. One of the key benefits to the company is that older employees take fewer days off sick from work, have excellent customer relations skills and are good role models and unofficial **mentors** for younger, less-experienced staff.

Key term

Mentor – trusted guide or adviser.

This is a perfect example of how we can learn from other people from different backgrounds at work. The older people recruited by Tesco will have a wealth of life experience to bring to their new role. This is evidenced by the fact that they often take on mentoring positions for younger staff. It is a natural thing for them to be able to do. Their excellent customer relations skills are the result of many years' experience of dealing with all types of people. It is this life experience which younger, less-experienced staff will not have. Tesco also found that older workers had a good influence on younger employees, who began to match their behaviour and good working ethos.

Like Tesco, many other organisations run recruitment campaigns targeted at older workers and also see good results. For example, the Co-operative Group is an Age Positive employer, having won an award for its diversity activities from the Age Positive initiative, which is a scheme run by the Department for Work and Pensions.

There are many other ways in which you can learn from others at work. For example:

- people who have done the same job as you for longer and have found the best ways of working and getting things done
- people from other departments who have a different experience base are often very valuable in offering advice on areas which may be new to you
- people from other cultures may have learned alternative methods for dealing with certain problems. For example, to shout and display anger is seen in some countries as a weakness. It is not considered acceptable behaviour and, consequently, is not normally seen in public. You may find it valuable, therefore, to learn from them their methods for dealing with frustrating situations or people.

Younger members of staff are able to benefit from a mentor's experience

Portfolio task 203.4 → Links to LO1: assessment criterion 1.4

Write a short report which describes ways in which it is possible to learn from other people at work. Include an example of how you have learned from another colleague at work in order to demonstrate your understanding of this.

How to maintain security and confidentiality at work

In this section, you will look at the reasons why it is essential to maintain security and confidentiality at work along with the benefits of this for the business.

Purpose of maintaining security and confidentiality

There are two main reasons for maintaining security at work.

- Under the Health and Safety at Work Act (1974) all employers have a duty to ensure the health and safety of all employees, and this includes being kept safe from harm and secure.

- A business's activities depend upon the security of its buildings, land, people, equipment and financial assets. If there is a breach of security in any of these areas, the business may be unable to continue its operations as normal.

The key reason for maintaining confidentiality at work relates to the protection of sensitive documents held by the business which, if made public, would damage the company. Such documents may contain information relating to the pay of its staff, the prices of new products or details of **proprietary** technology or other inventions unique to that company (imagine if a competitor got hold of this information). For some organisations, therefore, the protection of certain data from public view is critical.

The Data Protection Act 1998 also imposes certain requirements upon employers in terms of the storage, usage and access to data held on its systems. Businesses therefore have a duty to take certain steps to prevent unauthorised access to this sensitive data.

Benefits of maintaining security and confidentiality

These include the protection of staff, resources and sensitive data. If adequate systems and procedures are in place, the business has the security of knowing that its key assets are protected. Often, this involves a business's critical data and equipment.

> **Key term**
>
> **Proprietary** – something that is owned by a company and is not free for the public to use.

☑ **Checklist**

Protecting the business

Maintaining security and confidentiality at work is critical for the business. A breach of security or confidentiality could cause serious damage to a business.

Portfolio task 203.5   ➡ Links to LO2: assessment criterion 2.1

Write a report which describes the purpose and benefits of maintaining security and confidentiality at work and which could be used by your manager to help train new members of staff.

Requirements for security and confidentiality in an organisation

Security

For any business, it is essential to have adequate security arrangements in place to protect:

- buildings
- storage facilities
- equipment
- staff
- finances
- electronic data.

Alarm systems

Business premises can be protected with alarm systems. They should also have procedures specifying roles and responsibilities relating to the setting of the alarms, what to do in the event of an alarm being triggered and details and contact information for those who hold keys to the business premises.

CCTV

Security can be further improved by the installation of a closed circuit TV (CCTV) system, which should have sufficient cameras to view the vast majority of the premises. Nowadays, most businesses would consider this essential equipment.

Security guards

Another option for larger or more security-conscious businesses is the employment of a firm of security guards. Security guards can patrol the premises 24 hours a day and may require visitors to provide identification before they allow anyone access to the premises. Should an intruder be found, they may also be able to apprehend them immediately, rather than just watch the incident on CCTV after the event — and after the intruder has made off with goods from the business.

Confidentiality

All businesses must keep certain information confidential. This involves the protection of data and resources which are sensitive and which must be kept under strictly controlled access. Typically this would include:

- payroll information
- staff records including names, addresses and bank details
- customer databases
- new business ideas and products not yet available to the public
- intellectual property belonging to the company, such as new technology, or new inventions in development.

✓ Checklist

Intellectual property

Intellectual property (IP) includes not only physical resources but also ideas, words, songs, pictures, logos and software. All of these different types of IP need to be protected from unlawful copying.

All of these types of information require restrictions to be placed on their availability. For electronic data, a suitable user access-level privilege can be set, along with secure individual-user passwords. Computers containing sensitive data should also ideally be placed out of the sight and reach of other employees, usually in a separate office.

Paper-based information and files should be stored under lock and key, with only named individuals allowed access, and again, these should ideally be housed in an office away from the main staff area.

Portfolio task 203.6 → Links to LO2: assessment criterion 2.2

Write a list which describes requirements for security and confidentiality in an organisation. Include examples of items (business premises, computers, software) from your own organisation in your list, showing how security and confidentiality are dealt with for each item.

Legal requirements for security and confidentiality

The main legal requirement for businesses to observe in relation to security and confidentiality is the Data Protection Act 1998. The following section takes a closer look at what this means in practice and at how businesses can ensure that they comply with the provisions of the Act.

Complying with the Data Protection Act (1998)

The Data Protection Act (1988) governs how a business may use, process and store data about customers and staff. Any business that holds data on living people must comply with its requirements. The Act covers both electronic and paper-based data.

There are eight principles of data protection contained within the Act. Personal information (data) should be:

- processed fairly and lawfully
- processed for one or more specified and lawful purposes, and not further processed in any way that is incompatible with the original purpose
- adequate, relevant and not excessive
- accurate and, where necessary, kept up to date
- kept for no longer than is necessary for the purpose for which it is being used
- processed in line with the rights of individuals
- kept secure with appropriate technical and organisational measures taken to protect the information
- not transferred outside the European Economic Area (the European Union member states plus Norway, Iceland and Liechtenstein) unless there is adequate protection for the personal information being transferred. (Source: www.businesslink.gov.uk)

Failure to comply with the Act can result in severe penalties for a business and, for this reason, it is essential to ensure that all staff activity in relation to the use of personal data is carried out in accordance with these principles. There is a training need here – businesses must recognise that they are responsible for training their staff to be able to work within the requirements of the Act and know what they are and are not allowed to do.

✓ Checklist
Protecting personal data

The Data Protection Act refers not only to computer records but also to paper files, so it is equally important to protect these documents.

Portfolio task 203.7 → Links to LO2: assessment criterion 2.3

Write a short summary which describes the main legal requirements for security and confidentiality in businesses. Remember to look back over the requirements of the Data Protection Act 1998 listed in the section above to help you.

Procedures for dealing with concerns about security and confidentiality

Organisations need to deal with issues related to security and confidentiality in the correct manner in order to eliminate doubts and concerns and to prevent them developing into something more serious and to maintain the good reputation of the company.

For example, a customer of an online retailer may be concerned about entering personal information, including credit card details, into the website for fear of their details being passed on to third parties or misused in some way. The business should address this by having a publicly available policy on the use of personal data which it should put on the website alongside the area where the customer enters their data, so it is visible to them.

Normally, online retailers also explain their policy on the use of personal data in the confirmation email which is sent out to customers immediately after they have made a purchase from a website. This should serve to reassure customers as to the protection and security of their personal information.

Actions you should take to deal with security concerns

It is likely that you will come across situations where you are either informed of a suspected security problem or else you spot one yourself. As a key member of your department, you are responsible for taking appropriate action in every case. You cannot simply ignore such a situation. The best approach is always to report the issue to a relevant senior member of staff. This will usually be your line manager, or there may be specific departmental managers who will deal with the situation. For example, a colleague may tell you that they think their computer password has become known to another staff member. In this situation, you are responsible for informing your IT manager, if there is one, or your line manager, in order that the password can be reset immediately.

Portfolio task 203.8

→ Links to LO2: assessment criterion 2.4

Carry out some research to find out about the procedures which your company has for dealing with concerns about security and confidentiality.

Write a short summary which explains these procedures.

Functional skills

English: Reading

You may be able to use your work for portfolio task 203.8 as evidence towards Functional English Level 2: Reading. You will need to keep copies of all of the different documents which you read in order to prepare to write your answer. You need to demonstrate that you are able to select and use text from different sources to gather information and ideas and that you understood the main points contained in these documents.

Keeping waste to a minimum in a business environment

In this section, you will explore the issue of waste in businesses, and look at how and why everyone should be working to reduce this as far as possible. You will investigate causes of waste, different types of waste and the various options for waste reduction. For businesses that recycle their waste, there are many benefits. You will look at the various procedures to enable them to do this, and also at the impact that recycling has on both the business and the wider environment.

Purpose of keeping waste to a minimum

It is a fact of business life that waste is produced as a by-product of business activity. Two of the key questions to be asked of any business are:

● How much waste is currently being produced?

● What can be done to reduce this amount?

A waste audit

A waste audit is the starting point in any waste reduction initiative, as this will provide a baseline against which the business can measure its reductions. A business can carry out its own audit or it can enlist the services of one of the many voluntary or government-backed waste-management organisations to do this for them.

Why do we need to minimise waste?

● Waste represents a significant cost to a business, typically 4 per cent of turnover – this money could be better spent elsewhere in the business.

● By reducing waste, a business can reduce its **carbon footprint**.

● Minimising waste helps reduce the negative impact of the business on the environment.

● Less waste produced means that there is less to be sent to landfill sites, which is a key government target in the UK

● Waste is an inefficient use of resources, so any possible reduction in this and alternative uses to be found, demonstrates an improvement in efficiency – which is good for the business.

The waste management hierarchy – reduce, reuse, recycle

The hierarchy of waste management, which is shown in Figure 203.2, refers to the different ways of dealing with waste and identifies the best to the worst options in terms of environmental impact. The best option is to prevent any waste occurring and the worst is to have to dispose of an item.

Key term

Carbon footprint – the amount of carbon dioxide (CO_2) being produced by a business or individual.

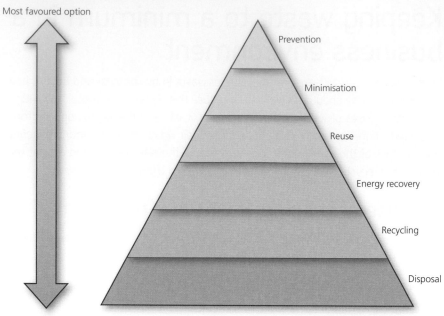

Most favoured option

Prevention

Minimisation

Reuse

Energy recovery

Recycling

Disposal

Least favoured option

Figure 203.2: *The waste management hierarchy*

✔ Checklist

Reducing waste

If a business wants to reduce waste, it needs to gain the support of every member of staff. By each person making small changes to the way in which they deal with resources at work and how they use and then dispose of them, huge reductions can be achieved by the business overall.

Portfolio task 203.9 → Links to LO3: assessment criterion 3.1

Produce a report which explains the purpose of keeping waste to a minimum. Try to show the different reasons why we should do this as well as the impact on our environment if we fail to do so.

Key term

Noxious chemical residue – unpleasant and harmful chemicals left over at the end of a production process.

The main causes of waste in the business environment

Businesses produce a variety of different types of waste, some of which are more easily recycled or disposed of than others. For example, waste paper is easily recyclable whereas **noxious chemical residue** is less easily dealt with in an environmentally friendly manner and is considerably more costly to dispose of.

In an office environment, such as the one in which you work, the main causes of waste are likely to arise from:

- paper used for printing and photocopying
- gas and electricity used for lights, heat and power to the premises and equipment
- water
- petrol and diesel fuels used in company vehicles
- cardboard used in packaging.

Printing and photocopying

Unnecessary printing and copying of documents and emails in offices accounts for a huge waste in paper. According to Waste Online, an information service managed by Waste Watch, a UK environmental charity, a recent study of the financial sector found that over half of the waste produced in company head offices was paper (Source: www.wasteonline.org.uk)

Paper usage can be significantly reduced either by using double-sided printing or copying, or by not printing non-essential documents. For example, rather than sending paper copies of a 50-page report to every single manager, why not send an electronic file instead? With just a little change to the usual practice, paper copies would then become the exception rather than the norm.

Many people automatically print out emails containing work tasks to complete. Instead, could they note them down in a diary or enter them into a computer-based task list or calendar? Think of how many sheets of paper you would save in a month!

Electricity

Think of all the things which electricity powers in an office. It provides, among other things, lighting, heating, and power for all computer equipment including PCs, printers, faxes, not to mention laminators and scanners. As you can see, electricity has a huge number of uses in the average office building.

Now imagine that all of these things are left on or running 24 hours a day, seven days a week, despite the fact that staff are in the office for only eight hours each day, five days week. Even without the use of a calculator, you can make a rough estimate that a huge cost saving – as well as a major energy saving for the environment – could be achieved simply by putting controls in place to turn off electrical equipment if it is not needed. Two-thirds of the electricity cost could be saved for the business. This would make a significant and dramatic impact on the annual costs for the business, money that could be diverted into other areas.

Water

Water is a scarce resource which is often taken for granted in the UK. We all have easy access to a plentiful supply of fresh drinking water every day, so it is perhaps not surprising that it is often overlooked in the schemes for waste reduction. However, it would take only one particularly dry summer to reduce water levels in reservoirs sufficiently for a drought warning and a hose pipe ban to be introduced. You can play an important part in thinking about water usage at work and taking steps to cut the amount of water you use.

The UK government's resource efficiency advisers, Envirowise, have estimated that 'UK businesses are collectively missing out on combined cost savings of as much as £10 million per day by failing to maximise the potential of water efficiency' (www.envirowise.gov.uk). Wasted water is therefore a huge cost for business.

Petrol and diesel fuels

In 2008, vehicles on UK roads accounted for 148 million tons of carbon emissions into the environment, so any reduction in this will be of major benefit to the environment. Carbon emissions are produced by vehicles burning fossil fuels (petrol and diesel) which, in turn, release carbon dioxide (CO_2), as well as other harmful by-products into the air. They are harmful to the environment because they create a cloak around the Earth, trapping heat. This cloak stays around for a very long time and the net effect is that it warms the Earth. According to the environmental pressure group, Friends of the Earth, the ten hottest years on record have occurred since 1997.

> Consider this. The average person in Africa emits 11 times less carbon dioxide than someone in the UK, and 21 times less than someone in the United States. So the real issue is high consumption of fossil fuels in richer countries such as the United States, Japan and, yes, the UK. Rich countries are home to just a fifth of the world's people but have pumped out four-fifths of the Earth's greenhouse gases since 1751. So it's up to rich countries to make cuts first — and fast.

Source: Friends of the Earth, 'How we can have a safe climate: 20 things you need to know about climate change'; www.foe.co.uk.

Greenhouse gas emissions in the UK

Look at Figure 203.3 which shows how much greenhouse gas was produced in the UK between 1990 and 2008. You can see at a glance that the three biggest contributors to greenhouse gas emissions are:

- business
- residential
- transport.

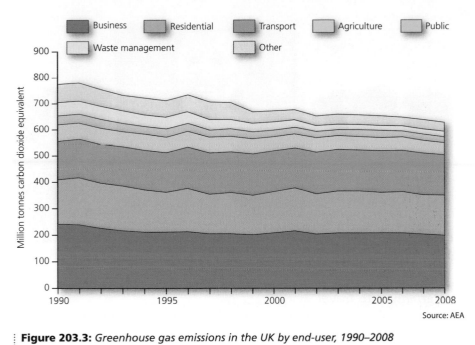

Figure 203.3: *Greenhouse gas emissions in the UK by end-user, 1990–2008*

Source: AEA

Here are some key facts on greenhouse gas emissions in the UK for 2008.

- Total emissions were 627.6 million tons in 2008.
- Business accounted for 198.7 million tons.
- Residential accounted for 152.6 million tons.
- Transport accounted for 150.1 million tons.

Source: Revised Statistical Release for end-user emissions estimates, 2008 results for UK greenhouse gas emissions and progress towards targets, Department of Energy and Climate Change, published 25 March 2010, updated 14 April 2010; www.decc.gov.uk.

✓ Checklist

Carbon footprint

The volume of greenhouse gas emissions produced by a business is referred to as its carbon footprint. Greenhouse gas emissions are the result of activities such as vehicles being driven on the road, as well as heat and light generated for the business. You can check out your own carbon footprint at the Carbon Footprint website. For a link to the site, please visit www.contentextra.com/businessadmin

In addition to the huge environmental impact, the cost of fuel in the UK is very high due to the amount of tax charged by the government, and this is in addition to the increasing costs of road tax needed for all vehicles. So, any business reducing its use of vehicles will not only help the environment but also make significant cost savings.

Business people in a video conference

Alternatives to travel

Simple, readily available and cost-effective alternatives to business travel include the use of video conferences and audio conference phone lines.

For the future, where travel is unavoidable, electric-powered vehicles may be the solution. These avoid the polluting effect of fossil fuels and are much cheaper in terms of road tax as well as fuel costs. Technological developments are making this a likely option.

Packaging

The use – and sometimes overuse – of packaging is a key contributor to waste in many UK businesses. By minimising or even eliminating packaging wherever possible, huge reductions in waste could be achieved.

Think about the average weekly supermarket shopping trip. Have you ever considered how unnecessary much of the packaging is? Many businesses are now actively reducing the amount of packaging that they use – notably the supermarkets – and using recyclable packaging wherever possible. All businesses should have schemes in place to reduce the amount of packaging used.

Portfolio task 203.10

➔ Links to LO3: assessment criterion 3.2

Carry out a search on the Internet to find out about the main causes of waste that may occur in a business environment. Using the information you find, produce a short report which describes the main causes of business waste.

Functional skills

English: Speaking, listening and communication

If you are asked to take part in a professional discussion with your assessor for portfolio task 203.10, you may be able to count this as evidence towards Functional English Level 2: Speaking, listening and communication. You will need to prepare for this discussion by making sure you are able to explain the main points in your report.

Ways of keeping waste to a minimum

These are some of the main methods used to reduce waste in an office environment.

- Set targets for reduction in use of paper, water, electricity and car mileage for staff, along with any other key waste areas. Appoint champions within the business to monitor and measure progress towards targets in each of the identified waste areas.

- Find eco-friendly ways to run the office. For example, place notices at key waste production points in the business to remind staff to take the correct waste reducing action: 'Please remember to turn off the power on your computer when you leave' or 'Do you really need to print this?'

- Divert waste products such as paper or card, plastic cups from water fountains and printer cartridges, into recycling sacks before they become waste.

- Set up contracts with eco-friendly suppliers for items such as print cartridge refills, photocopy paper, plastic cups – even stationery. Extending the waste reduction initiative in this way also shows customers how seriously the business takes its responsibilities.

- Ensure all staff are supportive of the schemes to reduce waste. Try running a competition either between departments or individuals, depending on the size of the company.

- Finally – and a very important way of motivating staff about the waste reduction activities – send a company-wide email once a month, updating staff on the latest figures and achievements in waste reduction measures and highlighting key individuals and departments who have carried out special activities or who have achieved targets in this area.

✓ Checklist

Practical tips for keeping office waste to a minimum

Everyone in an office can make small changes to the way they work in order to reduce the quantity of waste produced daily. Some practical tips for minimising waste include:

- Use the Print Preview function before printing a document, especially on a large-volume print run. This will enable you to make changes to your document and save wasted paper and ink.

- Use double-sided printing if this option is available in your office.

- Check documents carefully before copying. This will avoid them being put in the wrong way round and the job having to be redone.

- Check positions on the paper before doing large-volume stapling or hole punching. Find out if there is a machine available, or a print and copy service within your company, which can do this for you on large jobs.

What happens to our waste?

Much of our waste eventually ends up in landfill sites around the UK. These are huge holes in the ground into which rubbish is tipped. When full, they are covered with soil. However, with land in limited supply and an increasing population requiring more space for housing, there are fewer available sites for landfill. To tackle the shortage, the government imposed a landfill tax and this, together with initiatives for waste reduction and recycling, has led to a marked reduction in the amount of waste being sent to landfill.

There are currently 4000 landfill sites in the UK, so it is essential to find alternative methods of dealing with the huge quantities of waste which we produce each year.

Portfolio task 203.11   →   Links to LO3: assessment criterion 3.3

Produce a list which describes the main ways in which you can keep waste to a minimum. Remember to include any examples of waste minimisation from your own company.

Using technology to reduce waste

Technology can be used in surprising ways to help reduce waste. There are even companies that use waste reduction software to calculate the current cost of a business's waste materials and then produce an online plan to make drastic savings for the business.

Recycling means that less waste ends up in landfill sites

Use email instead of printing

A simple example of reducing paper waste in the office is the use of email and electronic documents, rather than paper. Also, notices asking staff not to print emails and documents unless it is really essential remind people to stop and think about what they are doing. Here is an example of a typical footer which could be set to attach to the bottom of all company emails:

'Consider the environment. Do you really need to print this email?'

Make better use of your company website

Directing customers and suppliers to the company's website to get the information they need, instead of sending them paper brochures, will help to save paper, print and postage costs (see Figure 203.4).

The company website could also be developed to take orders online, to order stock from suppliers and to invoice electronically. These procedures would otherwise involve paper, telephone and postage costs.

Install smart meters

Some companies have installed 'smart meters' to calculate the amount of electricity or gas being used by the business. Once initial usage levels are established, targets can then be set for all employees to achieve reductions, benefiting both the business in terms of reduced costs and the environment in terms of reduced carbon footprint.

Figure 203.4: *Use a website instead of paper-based brochures to save paper*

Case study – Severn Partnership cuts paper usage by 90 per cent

Here is how one firm has made an enormous saving on paper by adopting new technology in its business processes:

Severn Partnership was set up in 1983 and carries out surveys for clients in industries including railways, defence, airports and, more recently, golf courses and film studios for the leisure industry.

The Shrewsbury-based firm has seen the volume of paper it uses fall by 90 per cent after installing an online management system with the help of the National B2B Centre based at the University of Warwick.

The customer relationship management (CRM) system can manage all business applications and allows staff to use it as a database to log and track all jobs from initial enquiry to completion.

Source: www.nb2bc.co.uk.

Portfolio task 203.12
→ Links to LO3: assessment criterion 3.4

Write a short report identifying ways of using technology to reduce waste. Try to think of as many ways as you can. Carry out an Internet search to help you gather information.

Recycling

Recycling has a very important role to play, not just at work but also in every aspect of our lives. It involves diverting what would otherwise be classed as waste to other uses. So, the more you can recycle, the less waste there is to manage and dispose of.

Why should we recycle?

Businesses are currently being encouraged to recycle as much of their waste as possible. Typical materials from an office which are easily recycled include:

- paper
- cardboard
- plastic
- print cartridges
- mobile phones
- old computers and computer equipment
- metal.

All businesses and their employees need to be actively involved in schemes to recycle. This is because businesses should take responsibility for the waste products which they generate and manage their disposal in an environmentally friendly manner. This is an **ethical** concern. Why should the environment suffer just because of the activities and perhaps irresponsibility of a business? Think about it from a wider perspective and it is clear that this is a very important consideration.

According to the Ecology Global Network:

'Nearly 4 billion trees worldwide are cut down each year for paper, representing about 35% of all harvested trees. Fortunately, many of the trees used for paper come from tree farms which are planted and replenished for that purpose.'

Source: www.ecology.com.

Benefits of recycling

Individuals, communities, businesses and, ultimately, our planet all benefit from recycling. These are some of the key benefits.

- The more which can be recycled, the less is left over to go into landfill sites.
- Recycling saves money – this fact alone makes a very strong business case for it.
- Recycling enables us to create other uses for discarded items, saving us from buying new materials unnecessarily. We are also effectively getting more for our money out of one product.
- Recycling means we are not using up the earth's **finite resources**.

Portfolio task 203.13

→ Links to LO3: assessment criterion 3.5

Produce a notice to be displayed in and around your office which outlines the purpose and benefits of recycling. This notice should aim to encourage all staff to recycle as much as possible.

Functional skills

English: Speaking, listening and communication

If your assessor asks you to take part in a discussion about this portfolio task as part of the assessment for this learning outcome, you may be able to count it as evidence towards Level 2 Functional English: Speaking, listening and communication. You will need to prepare for this discussion by looking over your work and making sure you can explain the information which you chose to include in your notice. Also, be prepared to answer questions from your assessor.

Organisational procedures for recycling materials

All businesses should have procedures for recycling. A simple set of recycling procedures can be drawn up and included as part of the company manual. An outline of steps to be taken for each type of recycling should be included. It should be made a part of everyone's responsibility at work to be included in the drive to recycle as much as possible and staff may need training to raise their awareness.

For example, people need to know the types of materials that can be recycled and where they should be placed for processing. Recycling facilities need to be as effortless as possible to ensure that everyone uses them. Sometimes, it is all too easy to simply ignore the recycling procedures and put things into the general rubbish bin, especially if you are busy and the procedures are cumbersome.

An example of an organisation's procedure for recycling might look like the one shown in Figure 203.5.

Company Recycling Procedure

We are actively recycling the following materials:

- Paper
- Cardboard
- Plastic
- Print cartridges
- Electrical hardware
- CDs.

For each type of item, there is a special collection bin located in a designated position in the office.

Please make sure you place your recycling in the correct bin for collection. The recycling bins are collected once a month.

Figure 203.5: *Example of an organisation's recycling procedure*

✅ Checklist

Recycling procedure

A company procedure for recycling needs to include:

- a list of each identified type of recycling (plastic, paper, print cartridges, and so on), so that staff are aware of what is to be recycled

- a designated place where each type of recycling is to be placed ready for collection, usually a cardboard bin or sack

- information on when collections are made and company-wide email reminders the day before each collection. This will act as a reminder for people who may have recyclable materials at their workstation to put them in the recycling bins.

Portfolio task 203.14 → Links to LO3: assessment criterion 3.6

Write a short report which describes organisational procedures for recycling materials. Use recycling examples from your own company to help you. If your company does not take part in recycling schemes, carry out some Internet research to find out about the possibilities for office recycling and use these examples in your report.

Why is recycling so important in an office?

Office life

Jo's story

My name is Jo Clarke. I'm 22 and have been working as a personal assistant to the director of a company of architects for over a year. When I began work here, I was amazed by the volume of paper which was being needlessly wasted in the office and noticed that there were hardly any recycling facilities.

After a few months, I had compiled a list of key waste points around the company and I presented these in a brief report to my manager, along with my ideas for recycling and reusing items.

I was slightly apprehensive that my manager would think I was being critical, so I made a point of focusing the report on positive outcomes for the business and put the case as a simple cost–benefit exercise. This approach seemed to work. My boss liked the report and approved my ideas for implementing recycling initiatives.

I got to work setting up contracts with local suppliers, recycling companies and waste contractors. We implemented a company-wide recycling initiative, which had the personal backing of the managing director, and served to motivate everyone to take part. Within six months the company was already reaping the benefits of reduced waste costs and lower energy bills.

Ask the expert

Q My company is currently disposing of a vast amount of materials which could be better recycled or reused. How can I get the support of senior management to implement some green initiatives?

A A good starting point would be to carry out your own waste audit. This means looking in bins and skips, and watching out for unnecessary disposal of reusable or recyclable items. Look around for signs of energy wastage too. Finally, put your findings into a business-like report and show what can be done to reduce waste — measured in financial cost savings to the business as well as in terms of the obvious benefits to the environment.

Top tips

To minimise waste in your office, make sure everything is being done to either eliminate or reduce the amount of materials being sent to landfill. You can set up recycling schemes for paper, plastic and metal. There are also many recycling schemes which will remove your unwanted electrical equipment and furniture.

Other organisations may well have a use for your unwanted items. Use your local recycling exchange to identify these potential partners and give away unwanted items rather than disposing of them. You can locate your nearest exchanges by searching the Directgov website. For a link to the site, please visit www.contentextra.com/businessadmin

Finally, make sure energy conservation measures are in place around the office and that staff are supportive of them.

Procedures for disposal of hazardous materials

According to the Environment Agency, hazardous waste is defined as waste which is harmful to either human health or to the environment. Because this type of waste has potentially damaging effects once it is discarded by a business, it requires special treatment to ensure it is disposed of in a way which ensures it cannot cause harm.

The disposal of hazardous materials presents a challenge to businesses as they are legally bound to follow the correct procedure. Hazardous materials must not be included in the general rubbish.

Which types of material are hazardous?

There are a variety of different categories of hazardous materials. Some of these materials may be:

- flammable
- corrosive
- toxic
- carcinogenic (causing cancer).

Activity 2

Think about your organisation and try to identify as many potentially hazardous waste products as you can. Perhaps within the office itself, there may not be too many hazardous items, but if you extend your thinking to the factory or the warehouse, if there is one, you may find a surprising number of hazardous materials.

Within the office environment, printer toner is an example of a hazardous material because it is carcinogenic. You should therefore take special care when replacing a toner cartridge and be sure to wash off any toner which gets on your hands. Other examples include old computer monitors, fluorescent tubes from lights and lead-acid batteries.

✓ Checklist

Waste materials legislation

The two main pieces of legislation concerning waste materials are:

- The Hazardous Waste Regulations 2005
- The List of Waste Regulations 2005.

Benefits of procedures for recycling and disposal of hazardous materials

Businesses that produce hazardous waste materials are bound by law to take special measures in their recycling or disposal. They must have procedures in place to deal with hazardous materials and also to be able to monitor and review the company's use of such materials with a view to:

● eliminating some of these hazardous materials in favour of less hazardous alternatives where possible

● exploring all options for reuse and recycling rather than disposal.

There are several benefits for having a procedure to deal with hazardous materials.

● It ensures that the business stays within the law.

● It ensures that staff and visitors to the premises are kept safe from the harmful effects of these materials.

● It ensures the community and environment outside of the business are kept safe from the harmful effects of these materials.

● It reduces the company's costs associated with disposing of hazardous waste.

● It controls the flow of hazardous materials through the organisation.

● It will help to identify all of the options for reuse and recycling.

If a business did not have a procedure for dealing with hazardous materials, there would always be the risk that the materials could be disposed of in an unmonitored or uncontrolled way. For example, staff might dispose of hazardous materials in the wrong way and the business could be prosecuted as a result of this.

There are a number of professional agencies that can provide businesses with support, advice and guidance on matters relating to hazardous materials in the workplace.

While businesses must meet legal requirements, they can do more by producing less hazardous waste in the first place. This will benefit the company, as the costs of dealing with and disposing of such items will be lower. It will also benefit the environment.

Portfolio task 203.15 → Links to LO4: assessment criterion 4.1

Write a short paragraph which describes the benefits of having procedures for the recycling and disposal of hazardous materials.

Organisational procedures for the recycling and disposal of hazardous materials

Once a business has identified the hazardous materials that it uses, the next step is to decide for each one the most appropriate and cost-effective actions to be taken to deal with it.

Reuse, recycle, disposal

Remember, the best option available to a business is to reuse, second best is to recycle, and the last resort is to dispose of the item as hazardous waste.

Reuse

The business must reuse as many items as possible. Print cartridges, for example, can be refilled and reused. This not only avoids them going to landfill but it also saves the business the unnecessary expense of purchasing new cartridges – and it is significantly cheaper to refill pre-used cartridges. This is also an opportunity for the business to establish a good relationship with an environmentally friendly refill supplier.

Recycle

Whatever cannot be reused by the business should be recycled. There are many businesses and charities that will collect an array of items, from old office furniture to electrical equipment and old computers, to be recycled. Help is also available to businesses to locate partners to take away their recycling, as well as providing advice on waste management issues. Organisations such as Waste Connect can provide information and advice to businesses on these issues. For a link to the Waste Connect website, please visit www.contentextra.com/businessadmin.

Disposal

Disposing of hazardous materials is the last resort where items cannot be reused or recycled. These materials need to be sent to hazardous waste landfills and may need to be treated in order to reduce their hazardous nature or to make them safe to handle. There is a charge for disposing of this type of waste and certain types of waste may not be accepted depending on the landfill operator's permit.

Procedure for dealing with hazardous materials

A typical procedure for an office-based business might include the following:

- Nominate a person responsible for the management of hazardous materials within the business.
- Identify and list all of the hazardous materials which must be monitored.
- Establish the steps to be taken for dealing with each one (reuse, recycle or disposal).
- Specify the dates and times when external waste contractors and recycling companies will collect certain types of hazardous materials.
- Make sure all staff are aware of the procedure, the specific items concerned and the legal requirements relating to the management of these hazardous materials.

How much office waste can be reused or recycled?

Let's suppose that, in a typical office environment, hazardous materials consist of:

- printer toner cartridges
- fluorescent light tubes

- old computers
- lead-acid batteries
- other types of old electrical equipment.

As we have already seen, printer cartridges can be reused. In addition, all the remaining items can be recycled, so there will be nothing left over as waste to go to landfill. So, by simply following a good procedure and liaising with waste and recycling partners, a business can drastically reduce its waste costs.

Portfolio task 203.16   →   Links to LO4: assessment criterion 4.2

Write a short summary which describes your company's organisational procedures for the recycling and disposal of hazardous materials. If your company does not have any written procedures, ask others at work what it is that the company does. You can also carry out some Internet research to find examples of organisational procedures which you can include in your answer.

How to support sustainability in an organisation

If something is sustainable, this means that it can keep going. Therefore, sustainability is the ability of an organisation to keep going — to carry on with its business activities for the foreseeable future.

In a business context, sustainability refers to carrying out business activities in a way which does not cause harm to the environment. This includes making good where raw materials from the earth are being used up by the business. For example, if a company fells trees to produce paper to supply to businesses around the world, at some point in the future, there would be no trees left to fell. This is an unsustainable activity because it cannot keep going indefinitely. In order to make it a sustainable business activity, the company would need to replace the trees that it has cut down — it could do this by planting new trees.

Another way in which businesses attempt to become sustainable is by aiming to make their activities as ecologically sound as possible. This means reducing the use of resources to a minimum, using renewable energy instead of fossil fuel, reducing their carbon footprint and investing some of their capital into green initiatives.

Improving efficiency and minimising waste

In business, improving efficiency and minimising waste are interlinked ideas (Figure 203.6). To reduce waste helps to improve efficiency. If you improve efficiency, you are very likely to reduce waste.

Purpose of improving efficiency

Earlier in this unit, you learned that waste represents an inefficient use of resources and is therefore an unnecessary business cost which must be addressed.

A business must strive to improve efficiency as this is a key method of:

● improving business performance

● reducing costs relative to output

● improving productivity

● improving the financial and environmental health of the organisation.

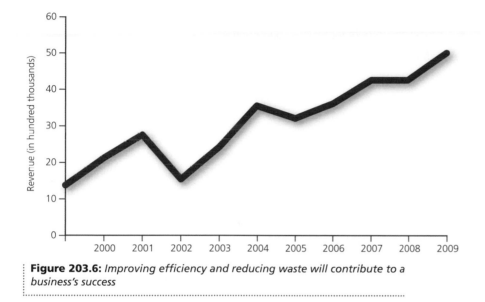

Figure 203.6: *Improving efficiency and reducing waste will contribute to a business's success*

Purpose of minimising waste

For a business, the purpose of minimising waste includes:

● reducing unnecessary expenditure on processing discarded resources

● focusing spending instead on useful initiatives which will provide a financial return for the business

● reducing the impact of waste produced on the community and the environment.

✓ Checklist

Minimising waste

To minimise waste means a business must recycle as much as it can. The more that can be recycled, the less is left over as waste, which ends up in landfill sites.

Portfolio task 203.17   → Links to LO5: assessment criterion 5.1

Produce a short report which outlines the purpose of improving efficiency and minimising waste. Give examples of how this would help your own company.

Improving working methods and using technology to achieve efficiency and reduce waste

There are many small changes you can make to the way you do things at work in order to improve efficiency and reduce waste. For example, in an office environment, you could:

● email documents rather than printing them

● use the company website to do as much as possible for the business, such as manage customers and suppliers online

● restrict the use of printing to a minimum — with the aim of becoming a paperless office (or as close to this as possible)

● go through your office's paperwork processes and remove all unnecessary printing and duplication. Instead, you could move to an electronic format. Documents can even be signed electronically nowadays, so there is no valid reason to have a 'paper trail', as long as secure backups are made of all electronic documents.

Longer-term plans for waste reduction

The changes listed above are things that can largely be put in place fairly quickly and with minimal expense. In the medium term, however, further changes can be made to the way the office is run. These will require approval from senior management as they will involve capital expenditure to set up. For example:

● Install motion sensors on lights in the office building. This will reduce unnecessary use of electricity for lighting, as lights will go out when no one is around.

● Make sure all unnecessary lights and heaters are turned off outside office working hours. This can be set up centrally.

● Use energy-efficient technology around the office — invest in low-energy consumption, eco-friendly computers and monitors

● Install a video-conferencing facility to reduce the number of miles which staff need to travel for meetings.

Portfolio task 203.18　　　　→　Links to LO5: assessment criterion 5.2

Describe ways of improving your own working methods and using technology to achieve efficiency and reduce waste.

Evidence collection

In order for you to complete the remaining assessment criterion to pass this unit successfully, you will need to carry out various tasks at work and then produce evidence to show that you have demonstrated the required skills and competence.

Evidence can be collected in a number of different ways. For example, it can be either a signed witness testimony from a colleague or line manager, a copy of any related emails or letters you have produced, or a verbal discussion with your assessor.

Speak to your assessor to identify the best methods to use in order to complete each portfolio task and remember to keep copies of all the evidence which you produce.

Respecting and supporting other people at work

For portfolio task 203.19, you will focus on gathering evidence for your assessor to show how you have behaved in ways that respect and support others.

Portfolio task 203.19 ➡ Links to L06: assessment criteria 6.1, 6.2, 6.3 and 6.4

Gather evidence of your work to show your assessor that you have successfully carried out the tasks outlined in the table below. Check with your assessor on the best ways of gathering evidence for each of the tasks before you begin.

Task	Evidence collected
1. Complete work tasks alongside other people in a way that shows respect for (a) backgrounds (b) abilities and (c) values, customs and beliefs.	
2. Complete work tasks with other people in a way that is sensitive to their needs.	
3. Use feedback and guidance from other people to improve your own way of working.	
4. Follow organisational procedures and legal requirements in relation to discrimination legislation.	

A version of this form, ready for you to complete, is available to download from www.contentextra. com/businessadmin

Maintain security and confidentiality

For the portfolio task 203.20, you will focus on gathering evidence for your assessor to show how you have behaved in ways that maintain security and confidentiality at work.

Portfolio task 203.20 → Links to LO7: assessment criteria 7.1, 7.2 and 7.3

Gather evidence of your work to show your assessor that you have successfully carried out the tasks outlined in the table below. Check with your assessor on the best ways of gathering evidence for each of the tasks before you begin.

Task	Evidence collected
1 Keep property secure, following organisational procedures and legal requirements, as required.	
2 Keep information secure and confidential, following organisational procedures and legal requirements.	
3 Follow organisational procedures to report concerns about security/confidentiality, as required.	

A version of this form, ready for you to complete, is available to download from www.contentextra.com/businessadmin

Support sustainability and minimise waste in an organisation

For portfolio task 203.21, you will focus on gathering evidence for your assessor to show how you have behaved in ways that support sustainability and minimise waste at work.

Portfolio task 203.21 → Links to LO8: assessment criteria 8.1, 8.2, 8.3 and 8.4

Gather evidence of your work to show your assessor that you have successfully carried out the tasks outlined in the table below. Check with your assessor on the best ways of gathering evidence for each of the tasks before you begin.

Task	Evidence collected
1 Complete work tasks, keeping waste to a minimum.	
2 Use technology in work task(s) in ways that minimise waste.	
3 Follow procedures for recycling and disposal of hazardous materials, as required.	
4 Follow procedures for the maintenance of equipment in own work.	

A version of this form, ready for you to complete, is available to download from www.contentextra.com/businessadmin

Check your knowledge

1 Which of these definitions correctly describes diversity?

a. Males aged 25–30 years of age only.

b. Employing older people in a business.

c. The many ways in which we are all different from each other.

d. Employment opportunities for 16–19 year olds.

2 In order to be able to mix with and get to know people from different age groups, religions, backgrounds and beliefs, what do you need to have?

a. An email account.

b. An extrovert personality.

c. An open mind.

d. An open door.

3 What does the Data Protection Act say that employers must do?

a. Employ people of all ages.

b. Employ more women than men.

c. Keep all personal data safe and adequately protected.

d. Keep all data on a spreadsheet.

4 What must you do if you are made aware of a suspected breach of security?

a. Do not mention it to anyone else in case you get the blame.

b. Email the receptionist to let them know about it.

c. Send a company-wide email letting all staff know about it.

d. Report the situation to your line manager or the manager responsible for dealing with security.

5 Why should a business aim to reduce its carbon footprint?

a. Because all businesses are doing this these days.

b. Because having a lower carbon footprint means fewer harmful carbon emissions are being released into the environment by the business.

c. Because carbon is no longer fashionable in business.

d. Because the business will get a good reputation if it does this.

6 Why is the government encouraging businesses to reduce waste?

a. Because UK businesses have too much money.

b. Because alternatives, such as recycling, need to be found in order to create a sustainable future.

c. Because waste management companies need to increase their business.

d. Because the government is refusing to deal with waste in the future.

7 What are the main causes of waste in most offices?

a. Time wasted by staff not working.

b. Miles travelled to and from meetings.

c. Paper used for printing and copying.

d. The cloakroom light accidentally being left on overnight.

8 What is a good method of encouraging your colleagues to reduce waste in the office?

a. Take the printer away so no one can print anything.

b. Ban all plastic cups.

c. Make people take their lunch wrappers and packaging home with them.

d. Place signs at key waste points reminding people only to use what they need and to put recyclable materials in the appropriate bin.

9 What is the benefit of encouraging staff to use email and electronic documents rather than printing?

a. It is easier to ignore emails.

b. It saves a huge amount of paper.

c. The printer will last longer.

d. Electronic documents are more colourful.

10 What are the key reasons for improving efficiency and reducing waste in a business?

a. To reduce costs and improve the overall health of the organisation.

b. To reduce unemployment.

c. To reduce carbon neutrality.

d. To pay less for paper.

Answers to these questions can be found at www.contentextra.com/businessadmin

Work in a business environment Unit Q203

What your assessor is looking for

Each unit in this qualification comprises two types of assessment requirements. These are:

- knowledge-based learning outcomes
- performance indicators.

In order to prepare for and succeed in completing this unit, your assessor will require you to be able to demonstrate competence in all of the assessment criteria listed in the table below.

Your assessor will guide you through the assessment process, but it is likely that for this unit you will need to:

- complete short written narratives or personal statements explaining your answers
- take part in professional discussions with your assessor to explain your answers verbally

- complete observations with your assessor ensuring that they can observe you carrying out your work tasks
- produce any relevant work products to help demonstrate how you have completed the assessment criterion
- ask your manager, a colleague or a customer for witness testimonies explaining how you have completed the assessment criterion.

The evidence which you generate for the assessment criterion in this unit may also count towards your evidence collection for some of the other units in this qualification. Your assessor will provide support and guidance on this.

The table below outlines the portfolio tasks which you need to complete for this unit, mapped to their associated assessment criteria.

Task and page reference	Mapping assessment criteria
Portfolio task 203.1 (page 58)	Assessment criterion: 1.1
Portfolio task 203.2 (page 59)	Assessment criterion: 1.2
Portfolio task 203.3 (page 61)	Assessment criterion: 1.3
Portfolio task 203.4 (page 62)	Assessment criterion: 1.4
Portfolio task 203.5 (page 63)	Assessment criterion: 2.1
Portfolio task 203.6 (page 64)	Assessment criterion: 2.2
Portfolio task 203.7 (page 65)	Assessment criterion: 2.3
Portfolio task 203.8 (page 66)	Assessment criterion: 2.4
Portfolio task 203. 9 (page 68)	Assessment criterion: 3.1
Portfolio task 203.10 (page 72)	Assessment criterion: 3.2
Portfolio task 203.11 (page 74)	Assessment criterion: 3.3
Portfolio task 203.12 (page 76)	Assessment criterion: 3.4
Portfolio task 203.13 (page 77)	Assessment criterion: 3.5
Portfolio task 203.14 (page 79)	Assessment criterion: 3.6
Portfolio task 203.15 (page 82)	Assessment criterion: 4.1
Portfolio task 203.16 (page 84)	Assessment criterion: 4.2
Portfolio task 203.17 (page 85)	Assessment criterion: 5.1
Portfolio task 203.18 (page 86)	Assessment criterion: 5.2
Portfolio task 203.19 (page 87)	Assessment criteria: 6.1, 6.2, 6.3, 6.4
Portfolio task 203.20 (page 88)	Assessment criteria: 7.1, 7.2, 7.3
Portfolio task 203.21 (page 88)	Assessment criteria: 8.1, 8.2, 8.3, 8.4

Unit Q204

Solve business problems

What you will learn

- **Know how to recognise business problems and their causes**
- **Understand techniques for solving business problems**
- **Know how to review approaches and solutions to business problems**
- **Be able to recognise business problems**
- **Be able to plan and carry out a solution to a business problem**
- **Be able to review a solution to a business problem**

Introduction

Identifying business problems — and finding solutions to them — is an ongoing challenge in any organisation, large or small. This is why people who are skilled in problem solving will always be in demand in business. In this unit, you will investigate how to recognise business problems and to identify their underlying causes. Only once you have done this will you be able to put together a plan for solving the problem.

You will examine several different techniques for problem solving and investigate the suitability of each technique for different types of problems. You will have the chance to use these techniques for yourself and to apply them to a business problem within your own organisation.

Finally, you will learn how to review different approaches to problem solving and understand the reasons why reviews are such an important part of the problem-solving process. Conducting reviews allows you to learn from your experiences and lets you consider which aspects you would use again — as well as those which you would not.

How to recognise business problems and their causes

Being able to recognise a business problem quickly and identify its root cause is a very good skill for you to develop and it will be valuable throughout your career, no matter where you work. Businesses always need key people who are expert problem solvers. This is because being able to spot a problem means action can be taken quickly to put a solution in place and to stop any further damage being done to the business. Let's begin by looking at ways of recognising when a business problem exists.

Recognising when a business problem exists

Business problems can occur anywhere within the organisation. They may arise, for example, from:

- staffing problems — these may be as a result of having too few staff, having too many untrained staff (so that the work is not being completed to the correct standard) or conflict between staff, making the office a very unpleasant place in which to work

- **resources** problems — these include having too few resources, old or outdated equipment or disputes between people or departments over who is given which resources

- financial problems — these may include poor end-of-year sales figures, high overhead costs, high raw materials costs or high costs of returned or sub-standard products (see Figure 204.1).

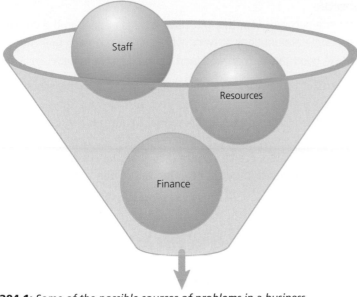

Figure 204.1: *Some of the possible sources of problems in a business*

The examples above are just a few of the possible sources of problems in a business. In fact, there are very many aspects of a business which can give rise to problems. All of these aspects need to be constantly monitored so that any changes can be quickly spotted and dealt with.

Is there a problem?

Some ways of recognising when a business problem exists include changes in:

- productivity
- **staff morale**
- number of people leaving the business
- company performance figures
- customer complaints.

Productivity

If there is evidence of a significant reduction in productivity, this is a key warning signal that something is going wrong. Good productivity is critical to the performance of a business because it means that there will be a high level of output per employee. In other words, people will be producing a lot of good work per hour or per day. If people are suddenly unable to keep up with their usual productivity rates, this will have a negative effect on the business as there will be fewer products produced (and therefore less to sell) while the business continues to pay the same wages to the same number of staff as before.

> **Key term**
>
> **Staff morale –** how happy the staff are. High morale means they are happy and low morale means they are unhappy.

Staff morale

If staff morale becomes low, this will have a huge impact on the quality of work. It means people are unhappy at work, which, in turn, means that they are less likely to take good care in their work and to be attentive to detail.

Imagine a customer service agent who was suffering from low morale. Since customer service agents deal with customers all day long, they need to be constantly positive, attentive and professional in all that they say. If they were feeling unhappy, it would not be long before customers on the other end of the phone noticed this. Also, customers are unlikely to be given the high level of service which they expect if the staff looking after them are unhappy.

Activity 1

Think of three other jobs where it is essential that staff are happy in their work. List them in the table below and, for each one, say what the consequences might be for the customers if staff morale is low.

Job title	Consequences of low morale
1	

A version of this table, ready for you to complete, is available to download from www.contentextra.com/businessadmin

Number of people leaving the business

If a business sees an increase in the number of employees leaving to go to work for other businesses, maybe even competitors, this is an indicator that there is a problem. Unhappy staff generally start to look for alternative jobs in the hope that they will be happier elsewhere.

You can measure the number of leavers per month or per year compared to the total number of staff to give you an idea of how your company is doing in retaining its staff. This measure is called **staff turnover**. If staff turnover is high, it means many people are leaving. If it is low, then people are staying with the company.

Let's look at an example of staff turnover to help you understand how it can be measured and what the figures mean. Suppose there are 1000 people employed in your company. Of these, 150 leave over the year. To work out the staff turnover figure, we use the following calculation:

$$\text{Staff turnover (\%)} = \frac{\text{Number of leavers}}{\text{Total number of staff} \times 100}$$

So:

$$\frac{150}{1000} \times 100 = 15\%$$

This means that 15 per cent of the staff leave over the year. This is a fairly low level of staff turnover and is an indication that staff for the most part are staying with the company.

Key term

Staff turnover – the number of people who leave a company over a year, usually expressed as a percentage.

Now let's compare this figure with the following example. Suppose that, of the 1000 members of staff, 600 leave over the year. That will give us a different picture altogether. Using the same calculation as above:

$$\frac{600}{1000} \times 100 = 60\%$$

Sixty per cent of staff leaving in one year is a high proportion and represents a high staff turnover. If this was the case in your business, something would need to be done to investigate why so many staff were leaving and plans would need to be put in place to try to lower this figure.

Activity 2

Think of two problems which your company would have to deal with if a large number of people started to leave. Write down your ideas in the table below.

Problems my company would have to deal with if large numbers of staff were leaving

A version of this table, ready for you to complete, is available to download from www.contentextra.com/businessadmin

✓ Checklist

Calculating staff turnover

When calculating staff turnover, divide the number of leavers by the total number of staff. Then, multiply by 100 to get your answer as a percentage figure.

Company performance figures

Company performance figures include sales, costs and **profit** for the year. If they show a marked decrease on previous years' figures, this can be an important indication that there is a problem somewhere in the business which is causing it to perform less well than before. It could be that its products and services are not as popular as they once were, or perhaps a new company is taking away business from the organisation, or that costs of raw materials are making production more expensive. Whatever the cause, the business must investigate it to find the problem and put it right.

Key term

Profit – total revenue (money coming into the business from sales) minus costs such as wages, raw materials and other running costs.

Unit Q204 Solve business problems

Customer complaints

The number of customer complaints which your business receives is a direct measure of how happy customers are with your products and services. As such, this is also a direct measure of how well your company is doing. If 30 per cent of customers are complaining about faulty products, this is a major problem which might put the company out of business if it is not dealt with quickly and effectively.

The average unhappy customer tells seven people, which is why it is so important for businesses to have excellent customer service staff.

Portfolio task 204.1 → Links to LO1: assessment criterion 1.1

Outline ways of recognising when a business problem exists. Use an example from your own organisation and say what the business problem was, along with what effect this had on the business. Finally, explain what was done to correct the problem.

How to identify possible causes of business problems

Once you have established that a business problem exists, you need to take action to discover its root cause. You have to begin by investigating the facts, then drill down to identify the cause of the problem before you can put a plan in place to correct it.

Figure 204.2 outlines a three-step approach to identifying possible causes of business problems.

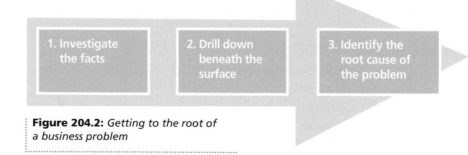

Figure 204.2: *Getting to the root of a business problem*

1 Investigate the facts

In order to keep a watchful eye on possible problems, you should regularly monitor the business's figures such as monthly costs. Analyse any **variances** from month to month. This is your starting point in getting to the cause of the problem.

Look at Table 204.1 and Figure 204.3 which show the costs for a business for the four quarters (qtr) of a year. You can see a steady increase in costs over the first three quarters and then a massive increase in quarter 4. This huge increase indicates that something dramatic has occurred in the business during these three months, and is the starting point for your investigation.

Key term

Variance – difference.

Quarter	1st qtr	2nd qtr	3rd qtr	4th qtr
Costs (£)	100,000	110,000	120,000	190,000
Increase from previous quarter	n/a	10,000	10,000	70,000
Percentage (%) increase from previous quarter	n/a	10%	9%	58%

Table 204.1: *Costs for a business over a year*

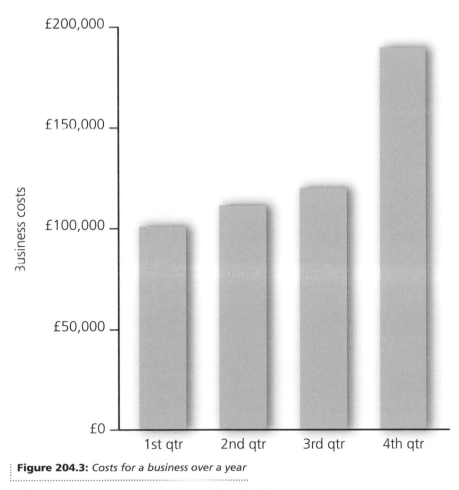

Figure 204.3: *Costs for a business over a year*

Unit Q204

Solve business problems

2 Drill down beneath the surface

Once you have looked at the facts, analysed the business figures and found where the problem lies, the next step is to go beneath the top layer of information to investigate the reasons for the increase. In the example above, the fact which you have uncovered is that there was a large increase in business costs in the last quarter of the year. In this case, you would need to:

- speak to the people who are responsible for buying the raw materials for the business to find out if they bought any extra **stock** during this time, and if so, why
- look at spending by each department to see where the highest spends occurred, and find out the reasons why
- identify any other unusual costs which arose at this time, once again seeking the reasons for this.

3 Identify the root cause of the problem

It could be that the business had to make a special purchase in that quarter which has produced such high figures for costs. Investment in new machinery or computer hardware, for example, would be expensive. However, the business would benefit from this investment for several years.

Figure 204.4 summarises the problem-solving approach used in this example.

Key term

Stock – supplies which a business keeps for future use and can include the raw materials to be used in the manufacture of products.

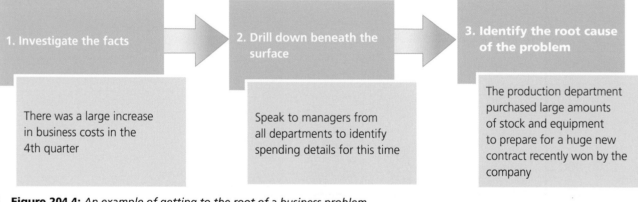

1. Investigate the facts
There was a large increase in business costs in the 4th quarter

2. Drill down beneath the surface
Speak to managers from all departments to identify spending details for this time

3. Identify the root cause of the problem
The production department purchased large amounts of stock and equipment to prepare for a huge new contract recently won by the company

Figure 204.4: *An example of getting to the root of a business problem*

A version of this table, ready for you to complete, is available to download from www.contentextra.com/businessadmin

Portfolio task 204.2 → Links to L01: assessment criterion 1.2

Describe how to identify possible causes of business problems. It may be useful for you to use the three-step approach outlined in this section on which to base your answer. Complete the table below to help you plan out your work.

1. Investigate the facts	2. Drill down beneath the surface	3. Identify the root cause of the problem
The problem is that …	This is happening because …	The root of the problem is …

Techniques for solving business problems

Developing a good understanding of how to go about solving problems in the workplace will give you valuable transferable skills in the jobs market. This means that you can use these skills in any job. It will also give you an advantage compared to other job candidates if you can demonstrate sound problem-solving ability when applying for more senior positions.

Different ways of solving a business problem

There are a number of tools and techniques which can be adopted in business in order to help you solve problems. The tools which you may need to use will depend on the size and complexity of the problem.

Simple problems may have an obvious solution which requires little or no analysis. Large or complicated problems, on the other hand, may need several different techniques to be used together to help you drill down to the root cause of the problem and, from there, identify the best solution.

Techniques which can be used include:

- SWOT analysis
- simple pros and cons evaluation
- the 5 Whys
- thought showers
- fishbone diagrams.

SWOT analysis

SWOT analysis is a template in which the strengths, weaknesses, opportunities and threats in a given situation can be listed. It is often used to help managers develop a **strategic business plan** for the organisation. SWOT analysis can also be used at departmental level or even for a single issue, such as how to improve efficiency in an office.

Table 204.2 shows a simple SWOT analysis that could be carried out for an **ethical** health and beauty chain such as The Body Shop.

> **Key terms**
>
> **Strategic business plan** – a plan for the long term, usually five years, which views the business as a whole.
>
> **Ethical** – having certain standards or principles. For example, The Body Shop attempts to carry out its business without causing harm to people, animals or to the planet.

Strengths	Weaknesses
• We have an excellent reputation and were one of the first in the market for ethically sourced beauty products.	• Other ethical producers have also entered the market over recent years.
Opportunities	**Threats**
• Develop new sales channels, e.g. the Internet. • Expand into other products such as clothing.	• Competitors may take some of our market share. • Similar products are now available from competitors.

Table 204.2: *Simple SWOT analysis for an ethical health and beauty chain*

> ### ✓ Checklist
>
> **SWOT analysis**
>
> When producing a SWOT analysis, opportunities tend to arise from strengths, and threats tend to relate to weaknesses.

A version of a SWOT analysis template, ready for you to complete, is available to download from www. contentextra.com/businessadmin

Activity 3

Using a SWOT analysis template like the one in Table 204.2, identify the strengths, weaknesses, opportunities and threats relating to how pleasant your office is as a place for you to work.

Simple pros and cons evaluation

A simple pros and cons evaluation is a good method to use for relatively straightforward issues. It is simply a list of the positives and negatives of a situation. The main benefit of this method is that it gives a basic, but very clear, overview of a situation from which you can then put together a solution.

If, for example, a manager was considering whether to buy new computers for all the staff in their department, they might use this technique to put together a simple list showing the positives and negatives of the situation – see Table 204.3. This will help identify a workable solution.

Pros	Cons
• Staff machines will run faster. • Screens will be easier to read. • Staff will be happier. • They will be able to get through more work.	• Cost of computers and installation will be expensive. • Installation will hold up people's work and disturb the department. • There may be additional costs such as software licenses to consider.

Table 204.3: *Pros and cons evaluation for buying new computers for the department*

Activity 4

Look at the pros and cons evaluation in Table 204.3. Do you think that the manager should buy new computers for all of the staff in the department? Give reasons to support your opinion.

The five Whys

This technique is used to drill down through the layers of a problem to get to a solution. It was first used by Toyota in Japan and has since been widely adopted by businesses all over the world. You can use this process for almost any problem. Have a look at the example in Table 204.4 to see how the method works in practice. You start with the problem, go through five rounds of asking 'why?' and then end up with a solution.

Problem	Your computer is very slow.
First why	Because the hard drive is full.
Second why	Because too many files are stored on it.
Third why	Because they have not been archived.
Fourth why	Because there is no procedure in place for archiving computer files.
Fifth why	Because you have been too busy.
Solution	Set some time aside and set up an archive for your computer files.

Table 204.4: *The five Whys in practice*

Activity 5

Now you are going to try the five Whys technique for yourself. Think of a problem or issue you would like to investigate. It can be something related to your own job or department, or it can be something from your personal life.

Use the following steps to guide you through the process.

- Start by stating the problem.

- Answer each round of the five Whys.

- Arrive at your solution.

A version of a 5 Whys template, ready for you to complete, is available to download from www.contentextra.com/businessadmin

Thought showers

Thought showers are an excellent method for generating lots of fresh ideas relating to a given problem. They yield the highest number of possible solutions of any of the problem-solving techniques.

This is an example of how a thought shower can work in practice.

- A team is gathered together in an informal setting.
- A leader is nominated.
- The leader puts the problem on a flip chart or whiteboard for everyone to see.
- All team members are encouraged to give their suggestions for solutions to the problem.
- Ideas are generated and developed by the team.
- Solutions are developed out of these ideas.

Figure 204.5 shows an example of a thought shower.

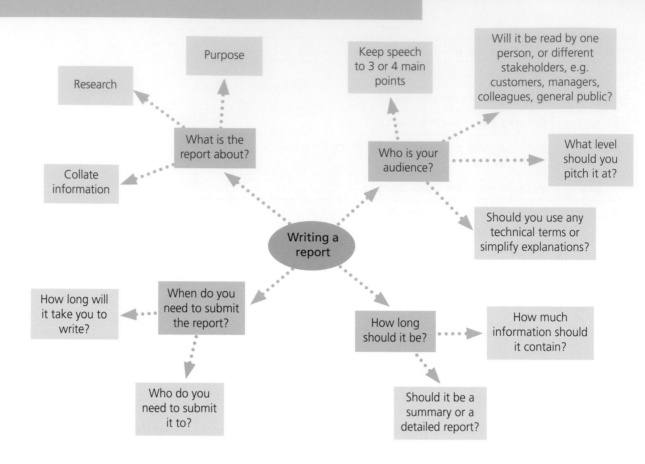

Figure 204.5: *An example of a thought shower*

A thought-shower session

For thought showers to work, people must feel free to offer any and all suggestions to the group — the aim is simply to get as many ideas on to the flip chart or board as possible. They do not have to be good ideas at this stage, as the ideas will be refined by the group later on.

✓ Checklist

Thought showers

When setting up a thought-shower session, keep the group size small, ideally no more than eight or nine people. People often find it harder to speak up in large groups.

Office life

Rachel's story

My name is Rachel Swallow. I'm 19 and have been working for a national insurance company as an office administrator for six months.

My manager has always encouraged me to be proactive in finding solutions to work problems, which is one of the things I like most about my job. So, when a group of us started chatting about how the office could be run much more efficiently — in particular, insurance claims seem to take a long time to process — I thought it would be a good idea to organise a thought-shower session with my colleagues in order to get them to give their ideas and suggestions of how we could make improvements.

My manager agreed and I organised a session with eight of us attending. I set up a flip chart at the front of the room and asked for everyone's ideas for improving efficiency in the office. To my dismay, hardly anyone spoke up and made a suggestion. The very same people who, in discussions in the office, had been keen to offer their ideas were now sitting quietly looking at the floor when I asked for input. I was becoming very worried about how I was going to explain this disappointing session to my manager.

Ask the expert

Q I recently ran a thought-shower session at work, but nobody wanted to speak up and give their ideas to the group. How can I get people to contribute more?

A When running a thought-shower session, you need to begin by explaining that any and all ideas are needed, no matter how offbeat or unconventional. The whole point of such an activity is to generate as many ideas as possible. It does not matter if they are good or bad, as the ideas themselves are not being judged — you just want as many of them as possible. In fact, you can encourage this process by starting the session off with an ice-breaker activity to get people talking to each other openly.

Top tips

To ensure a productive and lively thought-shower session, follow these important steps.

- No more than eight people per session. Large group numbers make it difficult for individuals to speak up.
- Tell the group that you want as many ideas as possible — no matter how wild or crazy they may be.
- Make sure people know that their ideas are not being judged for quality and that they won't be seen in a negative light for giving their opinions.
- A good thought-shower session needs a climate of openness and trust.

Activity 6

Now you are going to try a thought-shower activity of your own. The objective is to identify ways to help you ensure that you do well in your NVQ Business and Administration qualification. Write as many ideas as you can in the thought-shower template below – you have five minutes to complete the task! The first box has been done for you.

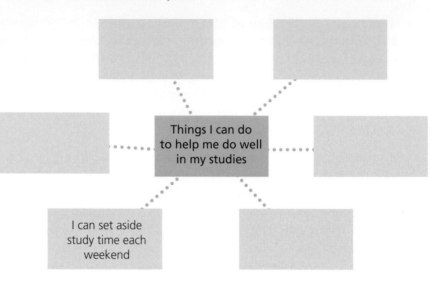

A version of the thought-shower template, ready for you to complete, is available to download from www. contentextra.com/businessadmin

Fishbone diagrams

Fishbone – also known as cause-and-effect – diagrams are a good method to use when you need to compile a lot of detailed information about a specific problem. You can write as much or as little as you like and extend sections of the diagram to suit your needs.

The process to put together a fishbone diagram consists of four steps.

1 Write down the problem.

2 List all of the factors involved with the problem such as location, people, processes, finances and any external influences which may be affecting the situation. Put each factor on a diagonal line stemming from the spine.

3 Once you have identified the factors, look at each one in turn. For each one, try to list as many potential causes as possible.

4 Review all of the factors and possible causes identified on your diagram. From these, you will be able to isolate what you think are the key roots of the problem.

Figure 204.6 shows an example of a fishbone diagram.

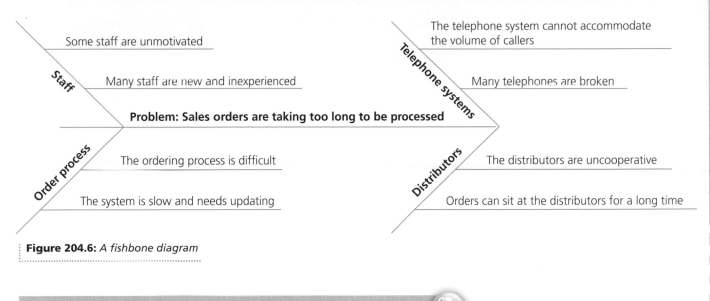

Figure 204.6: *A fishbone diagram*

Links to LO2: assessment criterion 2.1

Portfolio task 204.3

Describe different ways of solving a business problem. You may find it useful to select two of the techniques mentioned in this section and explain how each one would help you solve a business problem. Use the table below to help you plan out your answer.

Technique	How this could be used to help solve my business problem
1.	

A version of this table, ready for you to complete, is available to download from www.contentextra. com/businessadmin

Different ways of planning to solve a business problem

A problem-solving plan

An effective problem-solving process needs to be planned well. A plan will allow you to set out, in a logical order, all of the stages which you need to go through in order to get your solution implemented. It will also help to ensure that the solution chosen is the best option.

✓ Checklist

Problem solving

A plan is a framework for you to work within. It will make sure all of the essential activities are undertaken, with nothing being missed or left to chance.

The level of detail needed in planning to solve your business problem will reflect the complexity of the problem itself. It does not need to be highly detailed, but it does need to include certain key elements.

A plan is an essential first step in preparing to solve your business problem. Without one, you will have no framework within which to work. The following is an outline plan showing one way you could choose to solve a particular problem at work.

1   Define the problem.

2   Decide on the timing of the problem solving. Is the matter urgent, or can it wait?

3   Gather all the facts relating to the problem.

4   Consider and compare the possible options and decide on the best way to solve it.

5   Gather support from everyone whose cooperation you will need.

6   Implement the solution.

7   Monitor the results to see if they are as expected.

8   Refine the plan as needed in order to ensure results match up to expectations.

If the problem is very simple, you can have fewer stages or less detailed information in your plan. If, on the other hand, the problem is complex, you may wish to include more detail.

✓ Checklist

Problem-solving planning

Whichever way you choose to plan your problem solving, there are a few rules which will help you.

- Seek advice from people with experience in this area. You can learn valuable lessons from them.

- Base your plan on facts, not opinions.

- Think before you act.

- Consider the consequences of your plan before you implement it.

Key term

Task force – a special, expert team brought together to complete a specific task.

Planning methods for problem solving

There are many different planning methods you could use to solve a business problem. These are described below.

Setting up a task force

A **task force** is a special team which can include people from any area of the business and is set up with one aim — to solve the business problem. People are selected based on their skills and abilities in problem solving, so a highly effective team is created. Once the problem has been solved, the task force's members return to their normal jobs in the business.

A key advantage of using a task force to solve a problem is that there will be a good mix of skills and knowledge within the team and it will be very focused on achieving a good and lasting solution.

Using a team of managers and staff

Sometimes businesses use a team of managers and staff who are affected by the problem to find solutions to solve it. This is often part of a strategy of involvement and participation. The business benefits from highly detailed information from those working at the front line. Staff are able to discuss the core of the problem and are often the best placed to suggest the most effective and workable solutions.

Using an incentive approach

The business may offer an **incentive** to the team responsible for solving the business problem. This would usually be in the form of a cash bonus for completion within a set time limit. Any bonus may also depend upon the job being done within budget.

Hiring a team of outside consultants

Hiring a team of consultants from another organisation to undertake the problem-solving process is an excellent way to harness **expertise**. A key advantage is that the problem is handed over to experts in the field and they will offer the very best in management knowledge, with all the latest tools and techniques. They also offer an outside perspective. One disadvantage of using consultants, however, is that they are very expensive and, for this reason, only larger businesses would be able to afford their services.

> **Key terms**
>
> **Incentive** – something, such as a cash bonus, that motivates people to achieve higher results.
>
> **Expertise** – a very high level of skill in a certain area.
>
> **Stakeholder** – someone, such as employees or shareholders, affected by the actions of a business.

Portfolio task 204.4   → Links to LO2: assessment criterion 2.2

Outline different ways of planning to solve a business problem. It may be helpful to choose *one* business problem and produce *two* different ways of planning to solve it.

Support and feedback when solving the business problem

Support and feedback from your colleagues are essential for you when solving business problems. They will help you achieve an effective solution which suits the business.

Support

You will need support from all the **stakeholders** involved in the business problem in order for it to be successful. This will include senior managers and key decision-makers within the business. Support will provide you with the authority to be firm with your decision making and action planning.

Failure to gather all the necessary support from key people in the business will certainly make your work more difficult, if not impossible. Imagine if you wanted

Solve business problems Unit Q204

Key term

Cost–benefit analysis – a report which demonstrates the benefits of something relative to its costs. The aim is to show that it is worth the cost, as it will provide many benefits to the business.

to implement a plan to solve a basic problem in your office and your manager refused to support your idea. You would not get far at all.

How do you go about securing the support you are going to need? You must begin by gathering together your key support team and presenting your plan to them. Your presentation will need to be carefully put together and should be convincing and well reasoned. It will need to include a **cost–benefit analysis** or some other method of attaching a financial value to the solution to the problem for the business. Referring to the problem-solving approach in terms of financial benefit will focus the plan in purely objective terms.

✅ Checklist

'Buying in' to your solution

Getting support from key people in business is often referred to as getting 'buy-in' or getting people 'on board' with your idea. It will certainly involve some time and effort on your part to convince other staff of the benefits of your proposal.

Feedback

You will need to build in some feedback mechanisms to the problem-solving plan in order to gauge progress and results of the problem-solving solution. Accurate and regular feedback is the main way that will enable you to see how well the plan is working. It will allow you to make changes in your approach if the feedback indicates that your solution is not working. Figure 204.7 shows how feedback can be used to refine the problem-solving process.

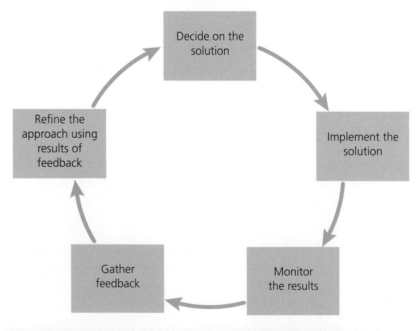

Figure 204.7: *Using feedback to refine the problem-solving process*

Feedback can be gathered through project team meetings, which can be scheduled at key milestones or stages in the problem-solving process. The information obtained can be reviewed and analysed immediately and, depending on the nature of the feedback received, any necessary changes can be put in place to refine the process and ensure it is creating a solution which actually works.

Individuals involved with — or affected by — the change can also provide you with feedback. This will give you 'grass roots' information on whether the project has had the planned result, or on where it might have failed. You will also find out first-hand how the people involved feel about it, which can highlight possible problems with a solution in time for them to be ironed out.

Gathering feedback from individuals can highlight whether a solution is a success or not

Portfolio task 204.5

→ Links to LO2: assessment criterion 2.3

Give reasons for having support and feedback from others when solving a business problem. Think of a problem which you have solved at work and say what the benefits of support and feedback were to you.

Checking progress and adjusting approaches to solving a business problem

When a solution to a business problem is being put in place, checking on progress and adjusting the approach being taken are very important activities which will keep the solution on track and ensure it works in practice.

Checking progress

It is important to check on your progress throughout each stage of the problem-solving process because you need to know that the decision you have made and the course of action you have chosen as a remedy to the problem are effective and achieving the desired results. Failing to check on progress could mean you continue with a poor course of action which damages the business further. In addition, if you do not check on progress, you cannot make any adjustments to your approach.

Methods for checking on progress include:

● setting review meetings for key milestones in the process

● using feedback mechanisms throughout the process

● setting **benchmarks** for certain times during the process which will set out where progress should be in terms of results achieved.

Key term

Benchmark – standard by which performance can be measured, usually set in terms of quality, cost and time.

Adjusting approaches

As a result of your progress checks, you may identify a need to make adjustments to the approach which you have chosen. This is a valuable activity as it means you are changing what you are doing in response to live data concerning the success of the project so far. Making adjustments in the light of results is critical to keep the project moving in the right direction. If you do not take action to make adjustments, the whole project could fail.

Portfolio task 204.6
→ Links to LO2: assessment criterion 2.4

Explain the purpose of checking progress and adjusting approaches to solving a business problem. Use an example of a business problem which has been solved in your organisation. Describe the way in which progress was checked and any adjustments which were subsequently made to the plan.

Recognising when a business problem has been solved

So, you have come to the end of your problem-solving process, the work has been completed, the process has ended. How do you know that the problem has been solved? This section examines some techniques to help you with this.

Analysing the facts

The first and perhaps most obvious approach to take in order to confirm that the problem has been solved is to do a fact-finding exercise. Start by going back to the beginning of the process when the problem was discovered. What was the problem? Look at the key issues. Next, carry out the exactly the same fact-finding exercise now. This is like a before-and-after snapshot of the situation. Compare the differences between the two.

Here is an example which may help to illustrate the process. The problem identified in a national call centre was that customer service staff were upsetting customers. Complaints were not being dealt with very well and a survey of customers of the business revealed that 75 per cent of them were dissatisfied with the way staff handled their complaint. The solution was to implement a customer service training scheme to help staff deal more effectively with customers' issues. In the latest survey of customer opinions, only 4 per cent were dissatisfied with the way in which their complaint was dealt with. You can see from this example that the solution has had a beneficial effect on the business. There has been a large reduction in the number of customers unhappy with how their complaint was dealt with. So, comparing the difference between the two sets of figures, the solution has worked in this case.

Asking staff for their opinions

Talking to employees in the business will give you a good guide as to whether the problem-solving process has been successful. Staff working on the front line can see for themselves how things are progressing more easily than managers, who are often one step removed from the detail of the process and only get this information later on.

Looking at customer complaints

A look at the business figures for customer complaints can often be an effective gauge as to how the business is currently performing. So, if complaints are low, then things are going well for the business. If, on the other hand, complaints are running at very high levels, you can see that there is a problem.

> **Portfolio task 204.7**   → Links to LO2: assessment criterion 2.5
>
> Describe ways of recognising when a business problem has been solved.

How to review approaches and solutions to business problems

You need to be able to review problem-solving approaches and solutions in order to establish whether they were effective. This type of investigation can only be carried out after the event because it is only at this stage that you will have all of the information which you need. You will be looking at these issues in more detail in this final section of the unit.

Ways of reviewing approaches

You will need to review the approach taken in solving a business problem to find out whether it worked and was effective or if there might have been a better approach which could have been adopted.

There are a number of ways in which you can conduct your review. These can include an investigation of the:

- costs of the approach taken
- time taken by staff involved
- techniques adopted to solve the problem.

Costs of the approach taken

The first review that you are likely to carry out will involve investigating the finances relating to the problem-solving approach. Look at the budget which was set. Now compare this with the actual costs. Did the project come in on budget or was there an **overspend**? If so, you will need to identify the causes. Could they have been accounted for in the initial budget? From this investigation, you will be able to avoid similar cost problems in future projects.

Comparing budgeted to actual figures is called **variance analysis**. If there was a significant variance between planned and actual spending, it is likely that this will have to be justified to senior management.

Reviewing approaches and solutions to business problems helps you to see how effective they were

Key terms

Overspend – occurs when a project costs more than the planned budget.

Variance analysis – a comparison of the budgeted figures with the actual costs that were incurred. This is carried out to see if there were any differences between the two sets of figures and to identify the reasons for this.

It is common in business for projects to come in over budget. This happens for a number of reasons.

- Things need to be added to the project along the way which were not known about at the outset.
- Additional people need to be consulted or drafted in to the project, which were not in the original plan.
- Key resources needed for the project cost more than planned.

All of these issues involve changes which become necessary once the project is already under way, so think about whether they could have been known about beforehand. If so, look again at your planning processes.

Activity 7

Projects very often come in over budget, and there are several well-known examples of huge projects which ended up taking longer to complete and costing much more than was originally planned. These include:

- the Millennium Dome
- the Channel Tunnel
- the Sydney Opera House.

For each of these projects, carry out an Internet search and identify exactly how much longer each took and how much more it cost than was originally planned.

It may help you to gather the information for your answer into the table below.

A version of this table, ready for you to complete, is available to download from www.contentextra. com/businessadmin

Project	Original estimate of time and cost	Final time taken and cost
The Millennium Dome		
The Channel Tunnel		
The Sydney Opera House		

Functional skills

Maths: Representing, analysing and interpreting

You may be able to use your work from Activity 7 as evidence towards Functional maths Level 1: Representing, analysing and interpreting. You will need to do some additional work however. For example, you could include another column in your table and, in it, calculate the percentage increase which occurred between budgeted and actual costs for each of the three projects. You may need some help from your assessor to complete this. Use this information to identify which project went the most over budget (a) in actual cost terms and (b) by percentage increase. Write a short summary paragraph which explains your findings and remember to check your writing for correct spelling and grammar.

Your assessor will help you to make sure you gather the correct evidence for your functional skills portfolio.

Time taken by staff involved

Another way to review the approach taken in problem solving is to analyse the actual number of hours input by staff in order to complete the process. You need to look back and compare this figure with the time estimates made at the beginning. If the time required by staff was much higher than you originally planned, it is possible that this will have affected their normal work by taking them away from it for longer than planned. You need to establish whether there have been any negative effects as a consequence of this. If staff had to spend longer than planned on the project, this will also have added a lot to costs. This is because staff time has to be costed per hour or per day and can be extremely expensive, especially for senior members of staff.

Techniques adopted to solve the problem

You will find it a useful activity to analyse the techniques which were adopted to solve the problem, such as SWOT analysis or fishbone diagrams, and review them for effectiveness. Look over the process which was involved and identify:

- whether the output from them was positive
- whether the ideas generated were workable
- whether the techniques chosen were the best ones.

Once again, by comparing what actually happened with what was planned, you can learn valuable lessons for fine-tuning future problem-solving approaches.

Portfolio task 204.8   → Links to L03: assessment criterion 3.1

Outline ways of reviewing approaches to solving business problems.

Reviewing the effectiveness of solutions

Reviewing the effectiveness of business solutions is the best way to determine whether they worked. A review will also tell you whether your solution was a lasting one or whether the results were short-lived. If you do not take the important step of conducting a review, you will not gather vital information which will help you with your next project. Learning from experience in this way ensures you will do better each time you are faced with a problem-solving activity.

Factors which make an effective solution

How do you know whether a solution to a business problem has been effective? Well, if a solution is effective, this means that it actually worked — in other words, it did what it was meant to do. So, if the problem was poor performance by sales staff, the effectiveness of the solution will depend on the quality of their performance afterwards. If the problem was too many defective products being manufactured on the production line, the effectiveness of the solution will depend on the number of defects occurring afterwards.

Effectiveness means a lasting solution, not just a short-lived fix to the problem. This means that you have to review results not just immediately afterwards but also over the following days, weeks and months.

A guide for reviewing effectiveness

The following is a simple action plan which will allow you to carry out a review of the effectiveness of your solution. It involves going back to the objectives of the problem solving and answering several questions. These will give you a good guide as to the success of your problem solving.

1   What was the problem? State the issue in simple terms.

2   What solution was implemented? Say what you decided to do to solve the problem.

3   What has happened since? Say what has changed as a result.

4   How can the improvement be measured? Establish how you are going to measure success. What are the factors which need to be monitored? How will you do this?

5   Is it **sustainable**? Say how you are going to measure results in the long term.

Key term

Sustainable – something that can continue for the foreseeable future.

Portfolio task 204.9

→ Links to LO3: assessment criterion 3.2

Outline ways of reviewing the effectiveness of solutions to business problems.

Evidence collection

For the remaining tasks in this unit, you will need to carry out various tasks at work and then produce evidence to show that you have demonstrated the various skills and competences listed below.

Evidence can be collected in a number of different ways. For example, it can be either a signed witness testimony from a colleague or line manager, a copy of any related emails or letters you have produced, or a verbal discussion with your assessor.

Speak to your assessor to identify the best methods to use in order to complete each task and remember to keep copies of all the evidence which you produce.

Check your knowledge

1 Business problems can emanate from many different areas, such as staffing, finance and resources. Which of these is an example of a staffing problem?

a. Staff morale is high.

b. Staff turnover is low.

c. Staff relations are good.

d. Staff morale is low.

2 If productivity improves in a business, this means that:

a. More people are leaving than before.

b. More raw materials are needed.

c. More is being produced with the same number of staff.

d. Less is being produced due to staffing issues.

3 What is a variance?

a. A difference.

b. Something which changes all the time.

c. An issue which is annoying at work.

d. A graph.

4 What does it mean if staff morale is high:

a. Staff are unhappy.

b. Staff are more likely to leave the organisation.

c. Staff are happy.

d. Staff are unable to use the new technology.

5 There are a number of techniques which can be used to help solve business problems. Which of these is *not* a problem-solving technique?

a. A SWOT analysis.

b. The 5 Nos.

c. A fishbone diagram.

d. Thought showers.

Answers to these questions can be found at www.contentextra.com/ businessadmin

6 What information does a simple pros and cons evaluation give you about a business problem?

a. It gives a complex diagram of the problem.

b. It gives a mathematical model of the probability of success.

c. It gives a simple overview of both the positives and negatives.

d. It gives you the answer to your problem.

7 What do the letters SWOT stand for?

a. Strong points, weak points, old points and technical points.

b. Strengths, weaknesses, other factors and what ifs.

c. Strengths, weaknesses, opportunities and threats.

d. Stationery, warehouse, options and theories.

8 Why is it important to check on progress throughout the course of a project?

a. To see who is not doing as they are told.

b. To see if the project is going to plan and to take action where corrections need to be made.

c. To save money.

d. To keep the boss happy.

9 What is a benchmark?

a. A notch on a bench which indicates that only the manager can sit there.

b. A standard for judging woodwork.

c. A type of manufacturing defect.

d. A standard by which performance can be measured.

10 Why is it important to be able to review the approach you took to solving a problem at work?

a. To prove that you were right all along.

b. To look back and see whether the approach worked as you had wanted it to.

c. To justify asking for a pay rise.

d. To make sure you can complete all the paperwork.

What your assessor is looking for

Each unit in this qualification comprises two types of assessment requirements. These are:

- knowledge-based learning outcomes
- performance indicators.

In order to prepare for and succeed in completing this unit, your assessor will require you to be able to demonstrate competence in all of the performance criteria listed in the table below.

Your assessor will guide you through the assessment process, but it is likely that for this unit you will need to:

- complete short written narratives or personal statements explaining your answers
- take part in professional discussions with your assessor to explain your answers verbally
- complete observations with your assessor ensuring that they can observe you carrying out your work tasks

- produce any relevant work products to help demonstrate how you have completed the assessment criteria
- ask your manager, a colleague or a customer for witness testimonies explaining how you have completed the assessment criteria.

The evidence which you generate for the assessment criteria in this unit may also count towards your evidence collection for some of the other units in this qualification. Your assessor will provide support and guidance on this.

The table below outlines the portfolio tasks which you need to complete for this unit, mapped to their associated assessment criteria.

Task and page reference	Mapping assessment criteria
Portfolio task 204.1 (page 96)	Assessment criterion: 1.1
Portfolio task 204.2 (page 98)	Assessment criterion: 1.2
Portfolio task 204.3 (page 105)	Assessment criterion: 2.1
Portfolio task 204.4 (page 107)	Assessment criterion: 2.2
Portfolio task 204.5 (page 109)	Assessment criterion: 2.3
Portfolio task 204.6 (page 110)	Assessment criterion: 2.4
Portfolio task 204.7 (page 111)	Assessment criterion: 2.5
Portfolio task 204.8 (page 113)	Assessment criterion: 3.1
Portfolio task 204.9 (page 114)	Assessment criterion: 3.2

Unit Q205

Work with other people in a business environment

What you will learn

- Understand how your role fits with organisational values and practices
- Understand how to work as part of a team to achieve goals and objectives
- Understand how to communicate as part of a team
- Understand the contribution of individuals within a team
- Understand how to deal with problems and disagreements
- Understand the purpose of feedback when working as a team
- Be able to work in a way that fits in with organisational values and practices
- Be able to work in a team to achieve goals and objectives
- Be able to deal with or refer problems in a team
- Be able to use feedback on objectives in a team

Introduction

All organisations, regardless of size or scale, rely on their most important assets, people, in order to be successful. Every person who works within an organisation has a particular role, or function, and supports the organisation as a whole to achieve its objectives or targets. As an employee, you will need to be able to communicate and work effectively with your team members and other colleagues, as well as external stakeholders such as customers and suppliers. This involves being able to implement widely accepted company practices to resolve complaints and disputes that may arise in the normal course of your working activity.

During this unit, you will identify where your role fits into the organisation that you work in, how your work fits into the jigsaw puzzle with the rest of your team, and how you all work together and support each other to meet the targets you are set. The unit also explores important issues such as whether you know what the rules and expectations of your organisation are, and how you implement them so that customers and other external stakeholders receive consistent service levels. You will need to be able to explain how you would deal with problems that arise, whether they are with customers or with colleagues.

You need to be aware of all the elements of this unit and be able to put them into practice so that you can become a more effective team member, and support your organisation to achieve its objectives.

How your role fits with organisational values and practices

At the end of this unit, you will need to write a guidance document for a colleague, which addresses all the assessment criteria for this learning outcome. As you work through each of the points of business theory, make sure you think about how they might apply to the organisation that you work in, as you will need to explain these in your report. Each portfolio task that you complete as you work through this section will help you to build evidence for the unit as a whole.

Sectors of industry and business ownership

Many people own their own businesses. These tend to be smaller companies such as hairdressers, newsagents or fish-and-chip shops. Some organisations are owned and controlled by larger numbers of people, called **shareholders**. Shareholders sometimes work within the company they own, and sometimes they simply make an investment but then elect **directors** to run the business on a day-to-day basis. Others are owned and controlled by the government on behalf of us all.

Key terms

Shareholder – a part owner of a company.

Director – a senior manager who is elected by the shareholders to make decisions and run the company on their behalf.

There are two different ways of classifying the sector that an organisation fits into:

- by economic sector
- by ownership.

You must use both ways, and also identify (or find out!) which categories your organisation falls into.

Economic sectors

Table 205.1 summarises the three main economic sectors. Think about your organisation and which sector it would fall into.

Primary sector	Secondary sector	Tertiary sector
The part of the economy that consists of agriculture, fishing and extracting raw materials such as coal.	The part of the economy that is concerned with taking raw materials and turning them into finished products, ready for sale. Often referred to as the 'manufacturing sector'.	The 'service sector'. Companies in the tertiary sector are concerned with providing customer service or intangible goods to their customers. This is the largest sector in the UK and includes banking, retail and hospitality businesses.

Table 205.1: *The three main economic sectors*

Who owns the business?

Private sector ownership

- Companies in the private sector are owned, run and controlled by individuals, sometimes called entrepreneurs, who have often taken the risk to devise an idea, and set up a company by themselves. If the company is successful, then the owners get their reward by earning a share of the **profit**.

- **Sole trader** – the smallest type of business ownership, where the business is typically owned by one person only. The owner might employ several people to work for them. Typical examples include plumbers, decorators and hairdressers. Owners of sole trader businesses are personally liable for all the decisions and debts of the business, so if a huge debt needs to be paid, the owner would have to sell their personal possessions in order to pay it. On the other hand, the owner can keep all the profit made for themselves, once they have paid the appropriate amount of tax.

> **Key term**
>
> **Profit** – the amount of money left over from a company's sales revenue once costs have been taken away (profit = revenue − costs).

Key terms

Share – a part of the business.

Dividend – a share of the company's profits. This is the reward that a shareholder receives.

Franchisee – a person or company who has bought the local rights to use the name, logo and brand image of another company.

Franchisor – the holder of the franchise who will sell the rights to use their name, logo and brand image to a franchisee in return for a share of the profit.

- **Partnership** — a company that is owned and run by two or more people who work together. The partners are jointly responsible for the success of the business and for running it on a day-to-day basis. Typical examples include solicitors, doctors and accountancy firms. In order to set up, partners need to draw up a contract called a 'Deed of Partnership' which sets out the rules by which they are going to run the company.

- **Private limited company** — this type of business ownership is easily identifiable by the letters 'Ltd' at the end of the company name. The owners are called shareholders and they each own a part of the company. The shareholders are usually friends and family. In return for their **share**, they receive a part of the company's profits at the end of each year. This is called a **dividend**.

- **Public limited company** — this is the largest type of business in the UK. A 'plc' trades its shares on the stock exchange and these can be bought and sold by anyone over the age of 18. Directors are appointed by the shareholders to run the company on a day-to-day basis. The ability to sell shares to anyone means that the company can raise large amounts of money to develop or expand its operations.

- **Franchise** — in this type of business, the owner pays for the right to use a well-known brand's identity. The **franchisee** pays the **franchisor** a share of the profit to use their logo, product range and then to benefit from the franchisor's promotion campaigns. The franchisee would also be given help and support to set up and run the company. Well-known examples include McDonald's, KFC and 'Tossed' salad bars.

- **Co-operative** — an ownership structure whereby the organisation is both owned and run by the same group of people. Each has an equal say in the decisions that are made and also enjoys a share in any profit that is made. The best-known co-operative in the UK is the Co-operative Retail Society (the Co-op) which is owned by its members (the shoppers).

Public sector ownership

Organisations that are owned and controlled by the state on behalf of the whole population of the country are in the public sector.

- **Government departments** — various different branches of the government have responsibilities for specific areas including education, health, benefits, taxation, defence and police, and so on.

- **Local authorities** — each local authority is given responsibility by central government to provide services such as refuse collection, road repairs, libraries and environmental care for its local community. As the needs and requirements of different areas of the country vary (countryside versus inner city, for example), it enables local decision-makers to address local needs.

- **Public corporations** — government-owned organisations such as the BBC are expected to operate in the interests of the country as a whole and, in this case, broadcast impartial views which help keep the public informed through news broadcasts, and so on.

Voluntary sector ownership

Organisations in the voluntary sector, also called 'not-for-profit' organisations, exist generally to raise money and give support to a particular cause, or people who require help. They are not allowed to generate a profit each year, but will look to make a **surplus** in order that they can spend money on supporting and promoting their chosen cause. Well-known organisations in this sector are charities such as Oxfam, the WWF, and Cancer Research UK.

Activity

Tesco's **strapline** is 'Every little helps ...'. What do you think this means? Why do you think the retailer includes it on all its promotional materials?

Key terms

Surplus – the money left over from donations once the charity has paid its expenses.

Strapline – a short, catchy phrase that a company will use to help strengthen its brand identity with customers.

Stakeholder – any person or organisation who has an interest in the activities of a business.

Mission statements, objectives and purpose

While a company's name is clearly very important, it must also communicate both to those who work for it and the outside world what is special about it and what it is aiming to do.

Just as you have a plan in your mind about the direction your life is going in (where do you see yourself by the time you are age 21? 25? 30?), companies do the same thing. They set a vision of the direction they are going in, and targets for where they want to be at various points in the future. By communicating elements of this vision to employees and other **stakeholders**, they try to make sure that everyone is working towards the same goals. Companies tend to call their goals or targets 'aims'. They break these down into manageable tasks called objectives.

Tesco's strapline 'Every little helps' is included in all its advertising

- **(Corporate) aim** – the long-term intentions that provide a focus for a company to follow. For example, the corporate aim of a chocolate manufacturer might be 'to produce the finest chocolate in the UK'. Aims form the basis for setting objectives.

- **(Corporate) objective** – medium- to long-term measurable/quantifiable targets that are set to help an organisation realise its aim(s)

- **Departmental objective** – measurable/quantifiable targets that help give each department within an organisation direction to help them to meet the overall corporate objectives.

Key terms

Corporate – of the company.

Unique selling point (USP) – the feature(s) of a product or organisation that makes it different from its competitors.

● **Mission statement** — a sentence that communicates the vision and purpose of the company. It is aimed at both internal and external stakeholders. The Body Shop's mission statement is 'Tirelessly work to narrow the gap between principle and practice, whilst making fun, passion and care part of our daily lives'.

● **Purpose** — the purpose of an organisation is 'the reason why it exists'. Does it offer particular products or services? Does it serve a particular community or part of a community? What is its **unique selling point (USP)**?

● **Responsibility** — the power to carry out particular duties within a job role (what you are supposed to do within your job role). The person with responsibility will be accountable (have to answer to) a supervisor or team leader.

Policies, procedures and systems

Policies, procedures and systems are in place in all organisations in order that all employees are kept safe, and carry out their duties in a consistent manner. They are also in place so that everyone within the organisation complies with the law.

All companies will have a health and safety policy, for example. This is required by law, under the Health and Safety at Work Act 1974, whereby an employer has an obligation to make sure that their employees are not at risk and are safe while at work. This obligation would include issues such as ensuring there are no sharp edges on furniture, or making sure that people who work at heights on ladders have been appropriately trained.

Other policies that companies might have in place include:

● recruitment and retention
● communication (email, phone, letter, and so on)
● customer service
● equal opportunities
● operational management
● attendance and punctuality.

Procedures and systems could include having a pre-defined way of placing orders for raw materials, or for processing a refund in a retail outlet. They are clearly set out ways of doing things within an organisation, and ensure consistency across the business. For example, if you visited a McDonald's restaurant in Worcester and ordered a Big Mac, you would expect exactly the same item and level of service if you were to go to a McDonald's restaurant in Exeter.

Values

The values of an organisation are the principles and ideals that it seeks to work to. For example, some companies such as the Co-operative currently subscribe to high levels of ethical and green values, seeking to combat climate change and only sourcing their meat from UK suppliers.

Values often dictate the culture of an organisation in terms of the way people in the organisation interact with each other. The values and the culture of the organisation will be reflected in the customer service that their employees provide, and what external stakeholders think about the company as a whole.

Portfolio task 205.1

→ Links to LO1: assessment criteria 1.1, 1.2, 1.3, 1.4, 1.5, 1.6, 1.7, and 1.8

Write a guidance document aimed at a new employee who has just been appointed to a role that is similar to yours.

The tasks below will help you to cover all the aspects that you cover in your document.

1 Write a brief profile of the company you work for, explaining who it is and what it does. You will need to include the sector of industry it is in, and the ownership structure.

2 Note down your company's mission statement, and what the company has identified as its purpose (why it exists).

3 Select *two* of your company's competitors. Write a brief profile of each, and identify two similarities and two differences between each of the competitors and your company.

4 Explain your job role (what you do on a daily basis and your main responsibilities). Explain also where your job fits into the hierarchy of the organisation. Explain also what you do as part of your job role that helps to ensure that the company as a whole runs smoothly, and keeps its customers happy.

5 Select *three* policies/practices/procedures that you have to adhere to within your job role. Explain them, and how they are relevant to your role.

6 If you were unsure about a particular aspect of your job, or needed further guidance as to what you might do in a particular situation, identify who you would need to contact (this may be more than one person, dependent on what procedure/policy it is).

When writing your guidance document, remember to structure it by including appropriate headings for each element, and use formal language.

How to work as part of a team to achieve goals and objectives

By the end of this unit, you will need to produce a diary and notes of meetings that you have had with colleagues, in order to produce the evidence for the assessment criteria for this learning outcome. As you work through each of the points of business theory, you will need to identify how working as part of a team unit is important, and how you might go about being an effective team member. Each portfolio task that you complete as you work through this section will help you to build evidence for the unit as a whole.

Key term

Motivation – the reason or incentive for an individual or group choosing to make a particular decision.

Working with other people to achieve goals and objectives

Working as part of a team is as simple as it sounds – interacting with other people in order that you can achieve a common goal together. The goal or target itself is not that important, but the fact that there is a group of people working together to achieve it means that there is often a higher level of friendship among the workers, and **motivation** to work harder for each other.

Benefits of teamwork

Working with other people often means that individuals feel 'wanted'. This sense of belonging encourages people to work harder for the team and so achieve better and more timely outcomes.

In addition, everyone within a team has strengths – things they are good at – and weaknesses – areas that they need to work on – so some members of the team will be better at some things than others. For example, you may be very good at talking to customers on the phone, and explaining to them that the contracts you have issued are detailed enough for the transaction; however, one of your colleagues may be better than you at organising the financial elements of the deal because of a job they have done previously that involved working in a bank. With this in mind, you could work with your colleague to close the deal and support each other to achieve the whole team's objectives.

Work goals and objectives

Each member of a team may well have their own targets that they are required to meet, based upon their particular expertise. However, the team as a whole will have an overall goal to work towards as well. For example, the strikers in a football team have a specific task to score goals. The defenders and goalkeeper might have a specific target not to concede any goals, and to 'mark' specific opposition players. The midfield might be charged with making sure that the strikers are given enough options and passes in order that they are able to attack the goal. Overall, though, the team would need to go out and win a match. All the elements of the football team, and the people within them, help the team to achieve its overall objective.

Quality of individuals and the team

The quality of the outcomes that each individual achieves will reflect on the entire team. Therefore, making sure that every team member's standards are high will ensure that customers are happy. If customers are happy they should return again and the reputation of the company will be strengthened.

Portfolio task 205.2   → Links to LO2: assessment criteria 2.1, 2.2, 2.3, 2.4, 2.5 and 2.6

1 Keep a four-week reflective diary, which explains examples of your experiences in the workplace. The diary should include a record of the date and time and a brief outline of the situation that you were part of, or witnessed.

   a) How can working with other people as part of a team help there to be positive/good outcomes? What could these outcomes be?

   b) Explain situations that you have experienced in which you have supported other members of your team, or they have supported you, to ensure that the job the team completed was to the highest possible standard.

   c) Describe the different ways that you have supported/helped members of your team, or how they have supported/helped you.

2 For this task, you will need to set up a meeting with your team leader to discuss the points below. During the meeting, you should keep a record of what you discussed, and write it up. Once this is complete, both you and your team leader should sign and date the document to prove that it did take place, and is an accurate record of the meeting.

   a) Why do so many organisations prefer their employees to work with other people in teams? Does it have an impact on achieving targets and objectives set?

   b) Why is it a good idea to agree targets and plan which member of the team is responsible for each job before getting started?

   c) Why is it important to agree *how* jobs are going to get done?

Office life

Peter's story

Peter Griggs, a retired chef, had been working full-time at the highly successful Tea and Scones café bar in Devon for about six months. He thought he was very good at his job making sandwiches and cream teas for the customers who came in each day. Jane, the café owner, seemed to be happy with his work, and was not aware that he did not have a particularly good working relationship with the part-time waitresses. Peter was getting increasingly frustrated with the waitresses' method of taking orders. He could not read their handwriting, so that he often made the wrong food. He would then react in an angry and slightly aggressive manner, telling them to rewrite the order, and shout at them if an incorrect order was returned by the customer. Jane was informed about the problems by one of her regular customers who was also a friend. She decided to observe the activities from both sides (waitresses and Peter) and then to talk to each of them to find out what they thought the problem was.

Ask the expert

Q What do you think the main problems in this situation are?

A The problem is clearly one of poor communication and a general lack of mutual respect between different members of the team resulting in poor customer service. Would the easiest way of solving it be to remove the 'problem(s)'? How do you know which areas the problems stem from? Jane should hold a meeting with Peter to understand his side of the problem, and then another with the team of waitresses. Once this is complete, she should then work with all her staff to set out a clear policy on how orders are to be communicated to Peter, and if there is a further issue then they are reported to her directly rather than argue in front of the customers.

Top tips

Peter should communicate regularly with Jane, so that they can train new waiting staff on how the chef would like orders communicated. In addition, the problems could be 'nipped in the bud' before they started having a negative impact on customers. The waitresses, as less-skilled employees, should be trained on the processes and procedures of the café by Jane and Peter *before* they begin work so that they are completely clear on the expectations and procedures, and ask any questions if they are unsure.

How to communicate as part of a team

By the end of this unit, you will need to produce a table of information that highlights different methods of communication that are used within the company you work for, and when they are used. You will also need to produce a corporate poster to explain to your colleagues *why* it is important to communicate with other people in the team.

As you work through each of the points of business theory, you will need to identify how communicating with the other members of your team unit is important, and how you would do it effectively.

Communicating with other people in the team

What is communication?

Communication is the way two or more people share information with each other. In order for communication to happen, the people who are sharing information must decide on a way of doing so (for example, having a telephone conversation).

Methods of communication

Communication methods can be electronic or non-electronic, written or non-written, as shown in Figure 205.1. Electronic communication methods use ICT, whereas non-electronic methods may be classified as more traditional ways of communication such as a face-to-face conversation. Written methods can be both electronic and non-electronic, while non-written methods are often electronic only.

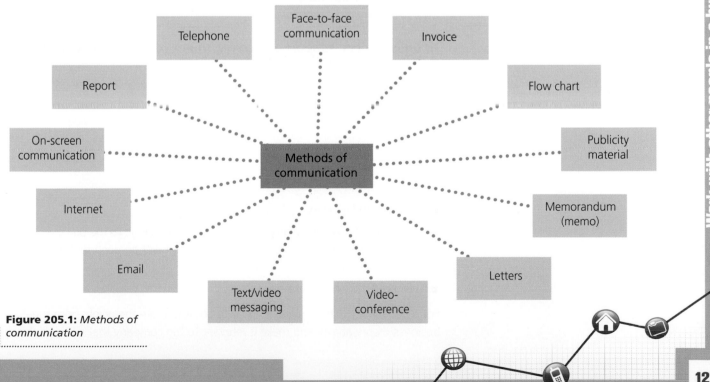

Figure 205.1: *Methods of communication*

Communication within a team is very important

Purpose of communication within a team

It is highly important that when communication between individuals in a team takes place, that the individuals can identify *why* it is happening, and what the intended outcome should be.

In the business environment you might communicate for the following reasons.

To check the understanding of the audience

As communication is about making sure that your audience understands what you have shared with them, it is often useful to devise a method of checking that they have grasped your message. This could be a simple question and answer session at the end of a talk, or perhaps a feedback form with questions on it. If your intended audience has not understood the message you are trying to put across, as a team leader, for example, the instructions and direction that you are expecting your subordinates to follow may not be completed to a high standard, if at all.

To seek clarification

Team members may check with others, or the team leader, to make sure they have fully understood the messages being given. This is not a sign of weakness, as managers far prefer to explain what is expected of you once more if that time spent would help to avoid a potential mistake in the future.

To respond to an impromptu situation

Team members who are confident, articulate and skilled communicators will have the ability to deal with questions, situations and incidents without any prior warning. This means that they are highly flexible, and will be able to respond positively to any unforeseen circumstances. If a team leader demonstrates these skills, then they will increase confidence within the team and the team may well work harder and achieve more.

To enlist others' support and commitment to the team's objectives

In order to 'get people to work for you', they will need to 'buy in' to your ideals and ideas. This way, they are more likely to support the goals of the company or team. The ability to get your colleagues to see your point of view and then to follow your lead is a highly important skill and requires the following attributes in order to be successful:

- strong interpersonal skills
- the ability to explain concepts clearly
- honesty and integrity
- the ability to explain clearly how your point, or change to the process, will benefit the audience – if they do not see how it will be good for them, they are unlikely to buy in
- the ability to persuade others.

For portfolio task 205.3, you will need to communicate the points from the business theory above, and make it relevant to the company that you work for.

Portfolio task 205.3 ➡ Links to LO3: assessment criteria 3.1 and 3.2

1 Create a display in the form of a table. One column should list methods of communication that are used in the company you work in, and the second should describe when each method is utilised.

2 Produce a poster to be shared with your team at your next meeting. Use the heading: 'COMMUNICATION! – we do it because...' Remember to use the corporate identity (logo, colour scheme, font style, and so on) of the company you work for so that when the poster is displayed, it 'fits' with the other company-wide messages. Also, give real examples for each point that you make, so that it is easier for your team members to understand what you are trying to explain to them.

The contribution of individuals within a team

All teams are made up of individuals who will bring the benefits of their own experiences to their work and contributions to achieving the goals of the team. Each individual will have their own strengths, and a diverse group of individuals who respect each other can often lead to positive outcomes for all concerned.

By the end of this section, you will need to give a presentation which explains why the strengths of individuals within a team are important and why having a **diverse team** is beneficial.

As you work through each of the points of business theory, you will need to identify why respect between all team members is important, and what your experiences of working in a diverse and mutually respecting team have taught you.

Recognising the strengths of others

The varying strengths of members within a team may include:

● communication skills
● the ability to present to large groups of unfamiliar people
● the ability to look professional when in a working environment
● listening skills
● empathy with other members of the team
● tact and respect for others
● previous experience of doing similar or the same type of jobs.

It is important to be aware of and embrace the strengths of members of the team and to realise when someone else may have more or better experience than you so you can draw on it. If you are a team leader, then delegating jobs is most effective if colleagues with more experience lead on areas of their expertise and use their skills to help train other members of the team.

> **Key term**
>
> **Diverse team –** a group of people who possess different skills, personality traits and attributes which, when combined together as part of a team, support the team's goals as a whole.

The value of diversity within teams

A diverse team will be one that contains a mix of different skill sets, ability levels, types of people, gender and backgrounds. They will possess a number of varied skills, at different levels of competency, and will be able to support each other. A gender mix (male and female) and wide age profile (young to old) will make sure that there is a spread of viewpoints and a balance between innovation and experience. If everyone in a team brought with them the same skills and characteristics, then it would be a boring place!

Respecting individuals working within a team

Respect is a quality that is free but which cannot always be expected. People earn respect for varying reasons: for being good at their job, for seeing the best in others, for valuing the contributions of all members of the team, for providing respect to others. It is highly important to respect team members for their individual positive characteristics, as it is all too easy to continually highlight the negatives or the fact that you may disagree with elements of your colleagues' personal viewpoints.

If personal and professional activities in the workplace are kept distinctly separate then conflict can be more easily avoided.

Portfolio task 205.4 → Links to LO4: assessment criteria 4.1, 4.2 and 4.3

Prepare a presentation which you could deliver to a group of people at a similar level in the hierarchy to your team leaders.

In order to highlight how you value the things that your colleagues are good at, you will need to give examples of particular strengths that individuals have, and why it is important for the whole team that there is a diverse mix of strengths.

You may wish to design your presentation in draft format, and then invite some of your colleagues/team members to preview it and suggest how you could improve your delivery or the visuals of the presentation itself so that you deliver a polished performance to your superiors.

How to deal with problems and disagreements

This section addresses your ability to identify and describe some of the different problems and disagreements that might occur as you work with others in a team. You will then need to explain the ways in which you might deal with these disagreements in order that the team can still continue to work effectively. You will learn about the different types of problems or disagreements that you may experience. At the end of the section, you will need to write a guidance document aimed at a colleague explaining what they might do if faced with a similar situation.

Types of problems and disagreements when working with other people

Most of the time, while at work, things will go smoothly and you will get on well with your colleagues. On occasions, however, there will be issues that arise between members of a team. It is important that you appreciate what some of these problems might be, why they might occur and how you might deal with them.

There are three main types of problems that could arise within a team.

Personality clashes

A personality clash is where members of the same team simply do not get on because their backgrounds and values are so different that they cannot **empathise** with each other. This can often lead to arguments in team meetings and may lead to spiteful comments or **back-stabbing**.

Personality clashes could occur because younger members of a diverse team do not have respect for their more experienced colleagues, and vice versa. The older members of a team will inevitably use their prior experience to analyse ideas, decisions and strategies and may not always appreciate ambitious 'upstarts' trying to make their mark. Conversely, younger colleagues might have new ideas or be more familiar with new technology and popular culture than older team members. Clashes often also occur between colleagues who are too similar in temperament and ambition. The two team members may be trying to compete with each other and disagreements can occur.

Authority clashes

Another type of problem that can sometimes occur is between team members who have a disagreement or issue with the team leader, or vice versa where the team leader clashes with a member of the team. These issues could relate to the fact that one or more members of the team are being paid at different rates, have different perks or fringe benefits written into their contracts or have been at the company for a longer period of time and therefore are treated differently.

Team members who either think they have superior knowledge to the team leader, or compared to their colleagues, may choose to act in a manner that makes those around them feel inferior. This behaviour can cause resentment

> ### Key terms
>
> **Empathy –** being able to appreciate how someone else might be feeling and why they might be feeling this way.
>
> **Back-stabbing –** where an individual is rude about a colleague, or takes action behind their back that may be harmful to them.

and stress among the rest of the team, and can compromise the team leader's position as their authority is constantly being challenged.

Workload clashes

Clashes with workload can often arise when more than one person has responsibility for a particular element of a project. There may be a lack of clarity as to who is responsible for the final outcome and therefore all colleagues assigned to it will want to do their bit towards the final piece. If the overall team leader has not delegated specific responsibilities, then more than one person may complete the same work or a task may be missed completely.

There may also be situations where team members are working on more than one project, or within two or more departments. Therefore their time is split between the various areas in which they are working. This might mean that deadlines could be missed or the core business of the projects could clash because one team member is being asked to take on too much work.

Ways of dealing with the problems and disagreements

Whatever the problem or disagreement is, it is advisable to think carefully before taking any action. There is no value in using the 'bull in a china shop' approach as this will usually make the situation worse.

It is important to take a step back from the situation and identify first of all if there is anything that you have done to either initiate or make the problem worse, and also to try to think back to when the issue first started. Once you have done this, you can work out a plan of action. This plan might involve:

- observing the situation and keeping a record of everything that happens for a two-week period
- talking to someone who is not involved (a trusted friend, perhaps) and asking for some objective advice
- talking the situation through with a colleague who feels the same way
- taking time to think about what might be the best course of action — this could involve passing on the information that you have.

The most appropriate course to follow will depend on the situation, and sometimes it is best to do nothing until you are sure that you have all the information and are clear in your own mind that you have the authority to take action.

Dealing with personality clashes

There are always people in the world that we just will not be able to get on with, no matter how hard we try to accommodate their thoughts, needs or ideas. In this situation, it is important to realise when you are in a team meeting for example, the way you put across your ideas is more important than what you actually say (a surprising amount of communication is non-verbal).

One strategy could be to see if you can find a common interest between yourself and your colleague (this could be work related, or part of your social life; perhaps to do with the football teams you support, or types of music that you like). This can often help to break down any perceived barriers. Over time, even those who may see you as competition will start to respect you for working hard. If you respect others as a matter of course, then these barriers can often be broken down.

If the personality clashes do not directly relate to you, then it might be that you choose to mediate between your colleagues if they ask you to. Alternatively, a strategy that you might use when the whole team is together is to keep the conversation moving along and away from the 'conflict topics'. This way you can remain outside the disagreement between your colleagues, at the same time trying to keep team morale at a reasonable level.

Dealing with authority clashes

Authority clashes can be the most difficult situations to deal with, especially if you personally have a disagreement with your team leader/line manager or a team member who is more senior than you. In the first instance, a positive way to try to sort out the situation is to arrange an informal meeting when no one else is around to try to clear the air. Should this not produce the result that you were both aiming for, it may be best to involve a more senior member of staff and ask their advice on what to do. They might also be aware of company procedures and have more experience than you in dealing with either that member of staff or potential conflict situations.

If the situation does not directly concern you, then you might choose either to ignore it or try to help resolve it. What you decide to do will very much depend on your position within the hierarchy of the organisation that you work in, and the level of authority/respect that you command from your peers and managers.

Dealing with workload clashes

Workload clashes should be the responsibility of the overall team leader to deal with. They may well have to liaise with other team leaders to ensure that the deadlines of employees who work in more than one team do not clash.

Should the issue be related to a lack of clear responsibility which has led to staff within a team duplicating work, if the members of the team cannot agree on who should do what, then maybe two or three members of the team should raise the subject with the team leader and ask them how best to progress.

Portfolio task 205.5 → Links to LO5: assessment criteria 5.1 and 5.2

1 At your next team meeting, watch how team members interact with each other, both through what they say and their body language.

2 Think about people at work who you have not managed to quite 'connect' with. See if you can identify the reasons for this and whether it could be a potential problem.

3 Based on a situation that you know well at work, describe two or three problems or disagreements that occur between members of your team, or another team. From what you have read above, and your own knowledge, suggest some methods of dealing with these problems. Present your thoughts as a mind map which should be colour coded so that you could explain it easily to someone else.

The purpose of feedback when working as a team

Whenever you are working with people, they are likely to ask for your opinion on ideas, processes (ways of doing things), activities and many other aspects of the team's performance. It is important to offer your thoughts and opinions in a sensitive way, so as not to offend any of your colleagues, while also putting your point across clearly. The feedback that you give needs to be purposeful and valid, rather than trying to simply pick holes in what a colleague is suggesting because you do not get on with them as well as you do with others. By the end of this section, you will be able to explain the purpose of giving and receiving constructive feedback, and also identify methods of using the feedback you receive to improve your own work and the work of the team as a whole.

What is constructive feedback?

In business, feedback involves expressing one's opinion on a colleague's work, highlighting the positives, and suggesting how to improve the weaker areas in order that the team/project objectives can be met.

The term 'constructive' means that the feedback you give, and receive, should be purposeful and help to achieve the project/team's objectives. Personal comments should be avoided — remember to be professional at all times. You should also provide feedback in the same way that you wish to receive it — there is nothing worse than spending hours completing a task, only for someone to come along and tell you that it is rubbish and you have wasted your time. Even if you want to say this, remember the 'bad news sandwich' — tell them something that they have done well, then tell them the bad news, then finish with something else that is positive.

The purpose of giving constructive feedback

Objectives

When commenting on other people's work, ensure that your feedback focuses on how they can improve what they have done to better address the objectives of the team or project.

Ultimately, the idea behind setting and reviewing targets is to ensure the final outcome is in line with the original vision of the project leader. Therefore, when providing constructive feedback to a colleague, ensure that it is clearly mapped against the original objectives. If someone in the team is working hard to complete tasks that they think are helping the team to move forward, but are actually going in the wrong direction, the team will find it increasingly difficult to meet its targets, and even bonuses could be at stake.

Supporting colleagues

Providing constructive feedback to support colleagues will help to ensure that they do not feel that they are working alone. When working as part of a team, a combination of formal and informal feedback (see below) is important to ensure that everyone involved knows that they can ask anyone for help, feedback or comments and they can rely on each other.

Knowledge, outcomes and processes

Sharing knowledge among team members means that everyone has a better understanding of what the team is working to achieve. If there are colleagues who do not fully understand the content, process or outcome of what is expected of them, or the team, then some support and feedback to give them direction will not only give them a confidence boost, because they will then know what they need to do, but also will bring the team closer together so that it works more effectively.

The purpose of receiving constructive feedback

In many ways, the purpose of receiving feedback is similar to giving it. The main difference is that by receiving feedback, and then acting upon it, you can improve your own performance, as well as supporting the team.

Improve performance

By listening to, and taking on board comments and suggestions from colleagues, you are able to better understand the job that you are doing, as well as what you can learn from those around you. This will enable you to become more efficient as you can learn from those who may have more experience, or different ideas, and benefit from them by being able to complete your job tasks to a higher level of quality, or in a shorter space of time (or indeed both).

Working closely with colleagues means you can support each other

By being guided to achieve the team or project objectives, you will naturally improve the performance and outcomes that you produce.

Colleagues supporting you

Working more closely with colleagues and other team members promotes a positive team spirit and will help you to support each other to achieve the team/project's objectives together.

Ways of using feedback to improve your own work and the team as a whole

Written or verbal feedback?

Written feedback, by email, handwritten comments on documents, sticky notes and so on, reinforces the improvements or positive attributes given during verbal feedback. While it might seem time-consuming, a combination of verbal and written feedback is beneficial because:

● the receiver can ask questions of the person giving the feedback which will help them to better understand the points being made

● written notes can help to jog the memories of both parties at a later stage. Think carefully about the colour of ink that feedback is written in, especially negative feedback.

Formal or informal feedback?

Formal feedback is generally delivered through a pre-arranged meeting or feedback forum. The discussion is usually recorded in writing and the actions for each party documented for review at a specified date in the future. This type of feedback may put the recipient under pressure, so it is advisable to pick the situation in which it is most appropriate.

Informal communication methods can be written or verbal, but do not have the sense of formality that a meeting, or feedback session, implies. Information feedback could be something as simple as a 'passing in the corridor conversation', or a chat over coffee in which an aspect of work is discussed. It is often more productive, and better received, especially if a more junior member of staff is making suggestions to a colleague with a higher level of experience.

As with anything else in a business environment, the specific action to take depends on the situation and people that are involved.

Improving your own performance

In order to use feedback to improve your performance, you will need to follow the process outlined below. (While the guidelines tend to focus on areas for improvement, they can just as easily be applied to good performance that needs to be maintained.)

1 Appreciation and acceptance — whatever your position within the team or organisation, you will receive feedback from colleagues about your performance. The only way of being able to use this to improve your performance is to *appreciate* the advice that is given and the spirit in which it is shared with you, and then *accept* the changes and/or improvements that need to be made. The level of appreciation and acceptance may stem from the role or status of the person giving you feedback. It might be from someone whom you do not get on well with. In this instance, try to take a more objective approach with a view that the outcome and change may well produce a better result.

2 Clarification — in order to act upon the feedback given, it may be that you need a completely clear understanding of either what you need to do or what the revised outcome should be. Ensure that any uncertainty is fully clarified with the person/people who are feeding back to you so that the task/process that you are refining meets the objectives set out.

3 Task and process — after both appreciating and accepting the feedback given, and also ensuring that you know what is expected of you, only then can the task or process be amended or improved. Before starting to make the improvements, it is important to set out a plan of what you are intending to do, and also then to have the objectives for the outcomes clearly set out. During the improvement stages, regularly check back with those who have given you feedback to ensure that the improvements are heading in the correct direction.

Portfolio task 205.6   ➡ Links to L06: assessment criteria 6.1 and 6.2

Produce a one-page document to be included in a supervisor/manager/team leader's handbook which explains how to give constructive feedback and how to take constructive feedback. Make sure that you include a few 'top tips' which explain why this is such an important process.

Work in a way that fits with organisational values and practices

For the learning outcomes so far, you have had to demonstrate understanding of the way in which you work with others as part of a team. For the remainder of this unit, you will need to gather evidence to show that you not only understand what you are supposed to do but also that you can do it. You will need to prove that your behaviour and working practices follow the policies, systems, procedures and ethos of the company that you work for. This means that everything that you do in your working practice must be corporate — in other words, fit in with how the rest of the organisation operates, whether you are dealing with colleagues, customers, suppliers or any other stakeholder. You must demonstrate that if you are unsure of how to approach a situation, you take appropriate action to find out.

Organisational policies, systems and procedures

As part of learning outcome 1, you demonstrated understanding of how your role fits into the organisation that you work in. For this outcome, you will need to show that you can actually work within the organisation's standard policies that you researched and demonstrate that you have fulfilled the competencies required for the role you have within the team and the organisation.

Organisational ethos and working within it

The ethos of an organisation is the values, beliefs and attitudes that are set by the leadership, and that all the employees subscribe to. It is essential that all employees work within the same boundaries. For example, Richard Branson of the Virgin Group and Julian Richer of Richer Sounds have created an ethos of creativity, team spirit and enterprise within their organisations. All employees operate in the same manner and strive to provide excellent customer service at all times.

It would be useful to use the corporate mission statement and aims to identify what you think the core elements of the ethos of the organisation you work for are. What kind of 'feeling' do you get each day when you are in the office?

Seeking guidance

However long you work within a particular organisation, you will never be completely sure about everything. Therefore, it is important to check with a colleague, whether at a similar or higher level in the hierarchy to you, if you are unsure about anything as regards carrying out your job. This might mean discussing a client conversation, meeting with a manager before the actual meeting or asking a trusted colleague to look over a document before you send it out.

Work in a team to achieve goals and objectives

To achieve this learning outcome, you will need to demonstrate that you can put into practice all the theory that you have understood about working in a team. This includes communicating effectively with colleagues, contributing to the team's work objectives and helping to achieve them, supporting other members of the team if they require it, respecting individuals within the team and ensuring high standards of your own work.

Evidence collection

The evidence for learning outcome 8 will come from your assessment of a project or assignment that you have recently been working on. You will be required to document *how* you have demonstrated the competencies outlined below.

Portfolio task 205.7 ➔ Links to LO7: assessment criteria 7.1, 7.2, 7.3 and 7.4; LO8: assessment criteria 8.1, 8.2, 8.3, 8.4, 8.5 and 8.6

Using a copy of your job description, give examples of how you have met your performance management objectives for the year. You may choose to do this by annotating your job description with examples of what you have done to fulfil each of the assessment criteria.

In your performance management review, explain how you dealt with external clients/customers/suppliers/ other stakeholders and maintained the ethos and values of the company you work for. Also explain how you sought support or guidance when you were unsure of how to deal with a particular situation.

To complete this task successfully, you will need to demonstrate that:

- you have followed/can follow the policies, systems and procedures of the organisation in order to complete your role – this includes acting within the ethos and values of the company

- when you have liaised or communicated with external organisations, you have maintained the high standards and ethos of the company that you work for

- you have asked for guidance/support/help when you needed it so that you could continue to maintain the high standards required of you

- you have communicated effectively with other members of your team in order that you all agree the objectives and standard of outcomes together and work towards them

- you have ensured that the methodology of completing the tasks required to achieve the team's objectives is undertaken in a way that uses each team member's strengths, and that support and guidance is regularly shared among the team so that each person is respected for their individual abilities

- you have ensured that time targets and agreed deadlines are met, and that your own work is of a high standard.

Deal with or refer problems in a team

Linking back to learning outcome 5, you are now required to put the theory of how you would deal with a problem or disagreement at work into practice. You will need to produce a case study of a situation that you were in, or have direct experience of, where things did not go smoothly. Taking into account what you have learned previously, and the role you have within the team, you need to resolve, or help to resolve the issue, and then make a decision whether it needs to be referred to a higher level or not. This will demonstrate that you not only know the procedure of what to do but that you can actually do it.

Unit Q205 Work with other people in a business environment

Portfolio task 205.8

→ Links to LO9: assessment criteria 9.1, 9.2 and 9.3

Following on from the mind map that you created in portfolio task 205.5, you now need to develop this by identifying in detail what you consider to be a significant problem or disagreement within the team that you are working in. You may find that it directly involves you or affects the way you work because of those around you.

If it directly affects you, in the table below note down the main issues, what you would like the end result to be, and the obstacle(s) to solving the problem.

The next step is to work out how to remove each of the obstacles. This may mean discussing the problem with some colleagues, gauging opinions from friends and family, doing some reflective thinking and looking in the policy and procedures handbooks at work.

You will need to keep a diary record and an **email audit trail** of the planning and problem solving that you do,

and the actions that you take. Remember that there will be a limit to how much you are able to solve yourself, as there may be some more serious issues that only team leaders or managers have the authority to deal with. In these instances, you must have evidence of a detailed email sent to the relevant person/people, giving details of your findings and what you have done so far. You must also explain why you are referring these issues to them.

Main issues	The obstacles to stop the end result happening are …	I would like the end result to be …

A version of this table, ready for you to complete, is available to download from www.contentextra.com/businessadmin

Key terms

Email audit trail – a record of all emails sent and received that can be used as evidence of discussion and agreement.

Use feedback on objectives in a team

The final section of this unit builds on learning outcome 6 in which you demonstrated understanding of giving and receiving feedback to improve the achievement of personal and team objectives. Now you will focus on providing and receiving constructive feedback to specifically identify whether the team's objectives have been met or not. You will then use this information to appraise your own work to improve your performance.

Portfolio task 205.9

→ Links to LO10: assessment criterion 10.1, 10.2 and 10.3

In order to achieve this learning outcome, you will need to act as the secretary for a team meeting where you are all present and discussing progress of a particular project/task/activity that you have all been working on. You will need to record the contributions that you make in terms of feeding back to colleagues on how their work has contributed to achieving the team objectives, and anything else that they could have done or done better to help reach the targets more comprehensively.

You will also need to record details of the feedback that you receive on your contributions to the team achieving the objectives set (make sure these are

detailed, because you will need them for the next part of the task).

Using the feedback on the achievement of your objectives, identify how you can improve your work and make notes on your work to remind you.

Using the feedback that you received about your own performance at the meeting, prepare a 'review statement' to explain, if you had to complete the same task(s) again, what you would do differently and why. Explain also what impact you think that the changes you plan to make will have on the overall outcomes of the task/project.

Check your knowledge

1 The tertiary sector is which part of the economy?

  a. It grows all the raw materials.

  b. It provides services and sells the final products.

  c. It turns raw materials into final products to sell.

  d. It supports consumers when they have a problem with suppliers.

2 What is a private limited company (Ltd)?

  a. An ownership structure whereby two or more people work together to set up and run a business.

  b. A company for which anyone can purchase shares on the stock exchange and therefore own a small part of it.

  c. A company that is owned and run by one person individually.

  d. A company that is owned by friends and family as shareholders.

3 Define the term 'voluntary sector'.

4 What does the term 'motivation' mean?

5 Explain two benefits of team working.

6 List four methods of communication.

7 Which of these are valid reasons for people within teams in an organisation to communicate with each other?

  a. To have a general chat about football or their social lives.

  b. To ensure that they fully understand the work that they are required to do.

  c. To liaise with each other to work on a project, and therefore help to meet targets or goals that are set.

  d. To pass a message to colleagues.

8 Which of the following attributes could be linked to a diverse team?

  a. A wide age range of team members.

  b. A team where all the members are 22-year-old women.

  c. A team of 12 people, encompassing five different religious backgrounds.

  d. An equal mix of male and female team members.

  e. Team members who have all had similar life experiences.

9 How could you address a disagreement within a team?

  a. Have an argument with each other in the middle of the office.

  b. Involve a neutral third party to mediate between both parties.

  c. Ignore the situation and hope that it will just go away.

  d. Arrange a mutually convenient time to sit down together and try to resolve the differences.

  e. Each party privately has a conversation with a manager to back-stab the other person.

Answers to these questions can be found on www.contentextra.com/businessadmin

What your assessor is looking for

Each unit in this qualification comprises two types of assessment requirements. These are:

- knowledge-based learning outcomes
- performance indicators.

In order to prepare for and succeed in completing this unit, your assessor will require you to be able to demonstrate competence in all of the performance criteria listed in the table below.

Your assessor will guide you through the assessment process, but it is likely that for this unit you will need to:

- complete short written narratives or personal statements explaining your answers
- take part in professional discussions with your assessor to explain your answers verbally

- complete observations with your assessor ensuring that they can observe you carrying out your work tasks
- produce any relevant work products to help demonstrate how you have completed the assessment criteria
- ask your manager, a colleague or a customer for witness testimonies explaining how you have completed the assessment criteria.

The evidence which you generate for the assessment criteria in this unit may also count towards your evidence collection for some of the other units in this qualification. Your assessor will provide support and guidance on this.

The table below outlines the portfolio tasks which you need to complete for this unit, mapped to their associated assessment criteria.

Task and page reference	Mapping assessment criteria
Portfolio task 205.1 (page 123)	Assessment criteria: 1.1, 1.2, 1.3, 1.4, 1.5, 1.6, 1.7, 1.8
Portfolio task 205.2 (page 125)	Assessment criteria: 2.1, 2.2, 2.3, 2.4, 2.5, 2.6
Portfolio task 205.3 (page 129)	Assessment criteria: 3.1, 3.2
Portfolio task 205.4 (page 130)	Assessment criteria: 4.1, 4.2, 4.3
Portfolio task 205.5 (page 134)	Assessment criteria: 5.2, 5.2
Portfolio task 205.6 (page 137)	Assessment criteria: 6.1, 6.2
Portfolio task 205.7 (page 139)	Assessment criteria: 7.1, 7.2, 7.3, 7.4, 8.1, 8.2, 8.3, 8.4, 8.5, 8.6
Portfolio task 205.8 (page 140)	Assessment criteria: 9.1, 9.2, 9.3
Portfolio task 205.9 (page 140)	Assessment criteria: 10.1, 10.2, 10.3

Respond to change in a business environment

What you will learn

- Understand the causes and effects of change in a business
- Understand own role in supporting change
- Understand own role in responding to change
- Be able to respond to change
- Be able to support the evaluation of change

Introduction

Change in business is something which is happening more and more in the current environment. The business world is becoming increasingly competitive, and driving down costs and making processes more streamlined is a key focus — and even a requirement — of every organisation in order to stay in business.

It is likely, therefore, that you will experience many types of change during your working life, as your career progresses over the years ahead. You will probably see changes in your own job role, an increasing use of IT systems, as well as changes in the way the office is administered.

You need to be aware of some of the possible causes of change and understand how they may affect you. Change can be caused by factors within the business itself (such as a cost-control exercise), or it may arise as a response to external factors which are not within the control of the business (such as a recession).

You will need to identify ways of behaving at work which support changes in processes and working methods. This is an important way of demonstrating your professionalism at work and your commitment to your organisation. It also demonstrates your ability to tackle new situations and use your initiative.

You will also consider ways in which you can deal with changes happening at work in order to understand why they are needed and to be able to respond to them in a positive way. This will ensure that you make the most of any opportunities which arise during your career as a result of change which occurs at work.

The causes and effects of change in a business environment

Change in business is necessary for survival. In a competitive world, any business which simply continues in the same way as it always did, without taking account of developments in technologies, fashions, changing consumer tastes and preferences, not to mention new products which competitors launch on to the market, is destined for failure. To survive in the long term, businesses need to be prepared to change to accommodate any and all of these issues.

Changes in working practices and why they happen

Next, you will investigate some of the changes to working practices that may occur, and some of the reasons for them.

Types of change

The types of change which can occur to working practices in a business, such as the one in which you work, could include:

- **automation** of routine office tasks
- replacement of paper invoices to customers with electronic invoices sent by email
- electronic storage of customer records, possibly even the setting up of an electronic **customer relationship management (CRM) database**
- **outsourcing** of certain administrative and support functions such as payroll, invoicing, human resource management or customer service; for example, many UK banks have moved their customer service function to call centres in India
- rearranging the way in which the business runs its central **support functions**.

Reasons for changes

Change can occur for a variety of reasons and may arise from issues within the business (internal triggers) or from the environment in which the business operates (external triggers).

External triggers for change

There are many external triggers for change (see Figure 227.1). These are factors outside of the business which force it to make changes to the way in which it operates. Examples include:

- The introduction of new **legislation**. Changes to the minimum wage, employment and health and safety legislation, as well as any changes to legal requirements in terms of product safety (which might cause a change in production methods or materials) will have an impact on the business.
- Changes in the market which affect the demand for a business's products. This could include the introduction of a new and better product by a competitor.
- Changes in consumer preferences. Consumers' likes and dislikes change over time and businesses must keep up with these changing preferences in order to keep their products popular. Failure to do this will see products losing sales and they may even become obsolete.
- The introduction of new technology. This could result in huge cost savings for the business, enabling it to make major gains in the market. Companies which fail to adopt new technology may be left behind and could lose their market position.
- Competition from abroad, where firms have much lower cost bases and can mass produce products much more cheaply than UK firms. Countries such as China, India, Malaysia, South Korea and those in eastern Europe are increasingly producing products cheaper and selling them into the UK market. This forces UK firms to cut their prices to compete.
- Changes in economic conditions, such as **boom** or **recession**, have a profound effect on business. In a recession, people have less money to spend and, as a result, are less likely to buy luxury items such as new cars or expensive clothes. Instead, they will keep their money for essential items. During a boom, on the other hand, people tend to buy expensive, non-essential items.

Key terms

Automation – using machines and computers, instead of people, to complete tasks.

Customer relationship management (CRM) database – special type of database which stores detailed information about a business's customers (including their purchase history and even their birthdays and children's names) so that products and services can be tailored to their individual needs and wants.

Outsourcing – giving a task or function to another company to perform for you.

Support functions – these include marketing, human resources, IT, sales and accounts.

Legislation – laws passed by the government.

Boom – a high point in terms of output and growth in the economy, where businesses are doing well, people are well off and have money to spend.

Recession – a downturn in the economy, where businesses are not doing well and people do not have much money to spend.

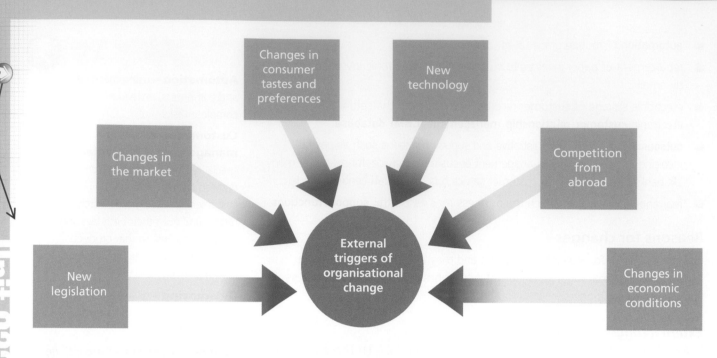

Figure 227.1: *External triggers of organisational change*

Internal triggers for change

Figure 227.2 shows some examples of the types of issues within a business which act as internal triggers for change. They include:

- new business activities, which may have been set up as a result of internal planning in order to generate more **revenue** for the business
- a drive to save money in certain areas, which could be a response to the poor financial performance of the business
- a need to reduce the number of staff that fulfil certain tasks
- a change in the way business functions are organised. The different functions, such as marketing, sales, IT, human resources, could be merged, split up or even outsourced to an external organisation in order to make them more efficient and cost-effective
- a need to acquire professional skills and expertise which the business requires but does not have. A good example of this is the acquisition of financial expertise by outsourcing some or all of the accounts function, often considered to be a cheaper option for businesses than having their own.

Key term

Revenue – money coming in to the business as a result of sales of its products and services.

✓ Checklist

Remember, internal triggers for change are usually things a business can control, whereas external triggers are not.

Figure 227.2: *Internal triggers of organisational change*

Unit Q227

Portfolio task 227.1

→ Links to L01: assessment criterion 1.1

Give examples of changes in working practices in a business environment, and explain why they occur. Use two examples from your own organisation and remember to give your own opinion as to why they are happening.

Functional skills

English: Writing

If you take care to produce a professional and well-presented report for your answer to portfolio task 227.1, you may be able to count it as evidence towards Level 1 Functional English: Writing. Remember to use headings and subheadings, check you have used correct spelling and grammar and then print out the final corrected version of your report, once you have made all of your corrections. Your assessor will help you to make sure you gather the correct evidence for your functional skills portfolio.

Effects of changes in working practices on people within a business environment

The possible effects of changes in working practices on the people who work in the organisation can be dramatic. They can be either positive or negative and this will depend upon the nature of the change, as well as the way in which it is implemented.

Key terms

Capital investment – money spent on items such as buildings, machinery, equipment and land. These are long-term purchases which will help the business to make money.

Working conditions – the work environment such as safety, hygiene, hours of work, break times and even possibilities of advancement.

Redundancy – when a business no longer requires staff and they lose their jobs.

Redeployment – moving staff from one part of the organisation to work in another part. This is done in order to make the business more efficient.

Positive effects on people

Change can be a positive thing and bring with it some welcome results. For example:

- It may bring about new ways of working which are more interesting, therefore increasing job satisfaction and morale.
- It may involve the development of new and exciting products which will improve the position of the business and provide more job security for its staff. The launch of Apple®'s iPad® in 2010 is a good example of this.
- It may involve **capital investment** in buildings and facilities which can provide a more pleasant work environment with better equipment and **working conditions** for staff.
- The introduction of new technologies into the business may mean staff are trained in the latest skills which means they are more valued by the business.

Negative effects on people

Change, unfortunately, may also bring unwelcome effects and new working methods which make life less enjoyable, at least in the short term, for staff. For example:

- It may result in some staff losing their jobs altogether.
- It may mean some staff have to work fewer hours and therefore earn less money as a result, with a negative impact on their quality of life.
- Staff may be forced to relocate to another area of the country in order to keep their jobs, or else face **redundancy**.
- Staff may be required to undertake new working methods and practices which are more mundane.
- Employees' old jobs may disappear as a result of organisational change and they may be **redeployed** elsewhere in the organisation. This might mean that they have to take on a new position which they may not like or want, perhaps even for lower pay.
- Staff may experience anxiety and stress as a result of changes taking place at work.

Portfolio task 227.2 → Links to LO1: assessment criterion 1.2

Describe the possible effects of changes in working practices on people within a business environment. It may help you to focus on one particular change at work and explain its effects on people, both positive and negative.

How change can benefit an organisation, team and individual

Change in a business brings with it many uncertainties from the point of view of the people working there. Nobody knows at the outset what the effects of the change will be for them until it takes place, which could take weeks or months. How will it affect their department? Will they have to move to another office and work with new people? Will they have to learn new systems and ways of working?

Office life

Jon's story

My name is Jon Macpherson. I'm 23 and have worked as an administrative assistant for a national engineering company for 18 months. I am the key point of contact for the engineers who are out on site visits most of the time and I am responsible for supporting the smooth running of all administrative tasks in the office, along with two other engineering assistants.

When I started work here, the office was fairly low tech, most things were done manually and all records were paper based rather than on computer. Shortly after, a new intranet system was introduced to store all of the office data electronically. The engineers could access the system wherever they were on site, and it greatly speeded up the processing of jobs.

However, we soon noticed there was a problem in finding and retrieving jobs in the system. The engineers were using different naming conventions for their files and, as a result, it was all but impossible for support staff to track their jobs and to complete follow-up administrative duties. It became apparent that the new system, which was introduced in order to improve efficiency across the business, was causing more problems than it was solving.

Ask the expert

Q We have recently introduced an electronic job-tracking system into our office. However, we are finding it very difficult to locate specific jobs within the system due to staff using all sorts of different file names for their jobs. How can we organise the jobs within the system so that we can locate them more easily?

A When a new system is introduced, everybody needs to be following the same rules regarding file naming so that there is a uniform approach to storing job data in the system. You need to decide on the best approach to file naming and ensure that all staff who need to use the system are aware of the correct way to name files and receive any necessary training. This way, everyone will be able to access the relevant files with ease.

Top tips

When a new system is introduced to a business, you need to think about how many people will be using the system to access the same files. A standard file-naming convention should be established throughout the business and checks should be made, in the initial phase after the new system is introduced, to ensure everyone is adhering to it. This is the only way that you can be sure files will be easily found by those needing to access them.

Key terms

Inefficiencies – aspects of a business that are generally wasteful, use too many resources or do not produce the desired results, for example outdated machines which run slowly and break down regularly or processes which take too long to complete.

Cost base – the very basic costs to keep a business running, such as wages, heating, lighting, water and rent.

Diversification – a business strategy to increase profits by entering new markets and selling new products.

Streamlined – working practices that have been refined and made as efficient as possible.

Despite the obvious uncertainties that change brings with it, there are many benefits which can be experienced at different levels – for the organisation, team and individuals.

Benefits to the organisation

Change at work can benefit the organisation in many ways.

- Stripping out **inefficiencies** from the business can mean a lower **cost base** for the organisation. Because the business's costs are lower, it can operate more efficiently.

- Increased profit may be possible where new procedures are quicker and easier to run, fewer people are needed and more output can be achieved using new systems and techniques. A good example of this is the computerisation of customer billing. If you have to complete this procedure manually, you must type up each bill individually and check it for spelling errors and correct billing amounts. If you move to a computer system for generating the bills, everything is automatically included, as all of the details are stored within one system, and you can produce hundreds of bills in a matter of minutes – instead of days.

- Where a business moves into the production of new products and services, it may be able to enter new markets, and this can be an effective way to grow the business and to strengthen its position, as it will be less reliant on any one particular product or market. This is called **diversification**.

- Better and more **streamlined** working practices can be established as a result of organisational change. This benefits the business as a whole because more efficient working practices will mean that employees are more productive which, in turn, means increased output for the business.

- A cleaner, more environmentally friendly business can be achieved by the introduction of green initiatives (as you have already seen in Unit 203 Work in a business environment). This can be of huge benefit to the business in terms of cost savings, as well as in establishing a good reputation in the community. It will also, of course, benefit the environment.

- Change can involve the building of new facilities, which will benefit the business in terms of its reputation as well as enabling economical business processes using cutting-edge technologies. It will also provide a more pleasant workplace for staff.

Ultimately, the goal of any business change, whether it is a small upgrade to a computer system, a rearrangement of the filing systems or a large restructure of the whole business, is to create improvements and hence a more secure future for the business – and for the people who work there.

✓ Checklist

Green initiatives in business include reducing the use of resources such as gas, electricity, petrol, paper and water. They also include recycling office items such as paper, plastic and printer cartridges.

Changes in working practices can greatly improve team morale

Benefits to the team

Teams can benefit from changes at work in a variety of ways.

● More resources may be made available for team working, enabling teams to be more productive.

● Team morale can be increased by changes in the way things are done if thought is given to working methods and their effects on team members. This is a very important consideration, as the way in which a job is designed has a great impact upon the morale of the person doing it.

● Team working initiatives may be given priority and rewarded with team bonuses for achievement of **key performance targets**.

● The introduction of new technologies may improve **team productivity** which, again, may increase team morale as people feel a greater sense of achievement.

● Teams may get a better sense of job satisfaction if changes are made that enable them to do their jobs better.

Benefits to the individual

The individuals who make up the workforce of an organisation can also benefit from changes in working practices.

● Improved working conditions can make work life more pleasant and enjoyable. Sometimes, even the smallest of changes to the office environment can have a major positive impact on working conditions. For example, suppose that in your office your desk was beside an old window that you could not open in summer but let in cold draughts in the winter. It had no sound proofing and your conversations and phone calls were constantly interrupted by traffic noise. Replacing the window with a modern, double-glazed, opening window would make life in the office much more comfortable.

● Individuals may receive training in new technologies, thereby increasing their skills base.

Key terms

Key performance targets – targets setting out what staff should achieve in their work.

Team productivity – the output of the team per day or per week. Teams tend to be more productive than individuals as they are able to motivate each other.

Unit Q227

Respond to change in a business environment

- Staff may benefit from increased morale as a result of changes which make their job more enjoyable. They are also more likely to stay with the company if they are happy in their work.

- Individuals may benefit from possibilities for further advancement in their career. For example, if new technologies are installed into the office or the factory, and staff are trained to a high level in their use, they may be able to progress towards a management position as a result of expertise in this new technology.

> ### ✓ Checklist
>
> It is widely accepted that staff who enjoy better working conditions are happier and more productive in their work. They are also more likely to stay with their employer for longer.

Portfolio task 227.3

→ Links to LO1: assessment criterion 1.3

Explain how change can benefit an organisation, team and individual. Try to include examples from your own company in your answer. Speak to colleagues and your manager to find out what changes have occurred in the office over the last year or two and their benefits. You can write about these and give an account of the experiences of your colleagues if you have not experienced any changes at work or been affected by them.

Functional Skills

English: Speaking, listening and communication

If your assessor asks you to take part in a discussion about this portfolio task as part of the assessment for this learning outcome, you may be able to count it as evidence towards Level 1 Functional English: Speaking, listening and communication.

Figure 227.3: *Training in new technologies can help individuals to advance their careers*

Your role in supporting change

In this section, you will explore the ways in which your role can be effective in supporting change in the organisation. You will look at how you can be actively involved in planning for change and at how you can prepare yourself for it in order to ensure a smooth transition to the new working practices. You will also investigate the types of support which you may need along the way, as well as methods for reviewing the effects of change on working practices.

Ways in which individuals can support change in a business environment

The success of any change strategy in a business is largely dependent on the staff and their acceptance of it. If the company introduces a new procedure but staff simply ignore it and continue as before, the planned change strategy simply will not work. Each and every member of staff has an influence on change and, as such, their cooperation and support is essential.

As a key member of your team, you will be expected to behave in ways which are supportive of the change. This will also have an influential effect on other members of the team. Things you can do to ensure you act as supportively as possible towards change include:

- volunteering to be first to undergo any new training which is needed, for example with the introduction of a new office system
- offering to train others in new systems and perhaps becoming first-line support once you have reached a sufficient level of skill
- always being positive in discussions of change with colleagues – this will enable you to maintain a professional approach to your work
- placing your own fears and misgivings to one side, or discussing them only in private with your manager
- embracing change, such as a new office move, as an opportunity for a fresh start rather than as a nuisance.

Other ways in which you can support the change process at work include being a positive role model for younger or less experienced colleagues who may be worried or unsettled. You can have a calming and reassuring influence on others and this will go a long way to ensuring a smooth transition to the new ways of working.

Portfolio task 227.4   → Links to LO2; assessment criterion 2.1

Describe ways in which individuals can support change in a business environment. Think about your own role and the things you could do in order to help ensure a smooth change in working practices.

Supporting the change process creates a positive work environment

Contributing to planning for change

The plans for making changes at work are a pivotal part of the change process and the better the plans, the better the implementation phase of the change. The quality of the plans, in turn, will depend to a large extent on the thought and effort which has gone into them, and this can be improved by inviting input from all of the people who are going to be affected by the changes (see Figure 227.4).

Figure 227.4: *Gathering input from those involved creates better plans*

Getting staff involved

Initiatives to involve all staff at the planning stage will reap enormous benefits for the whole process. If staff feel they are part of the planning process for change, they will be confident that the business is listening to them and will appreciate being asked their opinions. They will also enjoy seeing changes implemented at work which were, at least in part, their own ideas. They are also likely to contribute sensible, workable solutions of their own which senior management may not have considered.

Often, where staff are against change, this is for two main reasons.

- People are more likely to have a negative reaction to something when they have had no prior knowledge of or involvement with it.
- They are unlikely to be pleased about something which is being imposed upon them, rather than being carried out with their involvement and agreement.

Participation encourages a positive approach

If staff are actively involved in a change in process at work, they are far more likely to view it in a positive light, even where changes will have an effect on their own job activities. Being a part of the process for bringing about change will help employees understand why it is being implemented and enables them to see that the company is not trying to hide anything from them, which increases trust. Participation gives employees an insight into how the changes will work in practice, allows them to voice their concerns and to have these addressed in an open and honest exchange.

Participation and involvement are valuable strategies for creating a positive attitude and an atmosphere of trust. By participating in changes which are needed at work, employees have **ownership** of the change, to some extent at least, and are more likely to take on board issues which they would not otherwise.

Key term

Ownership – taking responsibility for something and having a willingness to work towards it.

✓ Checklist

Managers can help to maintain an atmosphere of openness at work by having an 'open door' policy towards their staff. This means that they are ready to listen to any member of staff if they have an issue at work.

Portfolio task 227.5 → Links to LO2: assessment criterion 2.2

Explain the purpose and benefits of contributing to planning for change. Use an example of a change which has occurred in your organisation to help you write up your answer.

Functional Skills

English: Reading

If you carry out research for this portfolio task, for example looking through books and the Internet to find relevant information, you may be able to include this work as evidence towards Level 2 Functional English: Reading.

You will need to keep evidence to show which books and websites you researched, and be able to summarise the contents of any useful texts which you found. Remember to keep copies of the names of the books and websites which you looked at, so that you can show these to your assessor. You will need to be able to demonstrate to your assessor how you used these texts to gather information and ideas for your portfolio task.

Your assessor will help you to make sure you gather the correct evidence for your functional skills portfolio.

How individuals can prepare for changes within a business environment

If individuals know about changes which are going to happen at work, they can take steps to prepare themselves in advance. It allows them time to consider how they can make the move to the new working situation as seamless as possible.

Some examples of changes which individuals may face at work include:

- **To prepare for a physical move to another office location**, you could first find out where it is going to be. You could organise your office belongings and equipment to make sure they are packed and ready for the removals team in good time for the move. Remember to label all of your boxes clearly.

- **To prepare for the introduction of a new system or piece of software**, you could ask for a relevant tutorial DVD and spend time working through this to familiarise yourself with the new technology. You can also request a training session to coincide with the installation so that you are up and running with the minimum of time lost.

- **To prepare for a transfer to another department or team**, you could find out who your new colleagues are going to be and then go and introduce yourself to them ahead of the move. This way, when you are due to move across, you will already be familiar with the people at the other end. You could also find out the location of your new desk while you are there and arrange for your things to be transferred before you are due to move. Have a look around and plan where you are going to put your things. Make a list of any items you will need and get them ordered in good time.

Portfolio task 227.6 → Links to L02: assessment criterion 2.3

In order to complete this portfolio task you need to show that you can explain how individuals can prepare for changes within a business environment and in ways of working. You can provide evidence for your assessment by completing the table below.

For each of the examples given in the table below, think about how you could prepare yourself in advance. List one thing which you could do to prepare for each scenario. Would you need help from anyone else? If so, mention this below.

Type of change	How you could prepare for it
A physical move to another office location	
The introduction of a new system or piece of software	
A transfer to another department or team	

A version of this table, ready for you to complete, is available to download from www.contentextra.com/businessadmin

Types of support that people need during change

Change in working arrangements, whether large or small, can be a time of uncertainty for the employees involved and they may need support to help them through the process. The type and extent of support will depend on the nature of the changes as well as the individuals concerned. Support requirements during a mass redundancy, for example, would be far more extensive than those for a simple software upgrade.

Some of the different types of support which can be offered by organisations include:

- emotional support and counselling — this may be appropriate where, for example, people are being moved to another role or location which they have not chosen themselves
- IT support — training in new working systems may be needed where an individual's job has changed to involve new or different technologies
- redundancy support — this is a specialist type of service offered in cases where the organisation has had to let some of its staff go. It may include help in applying for new jobs.

Portfolio task 227.7 → Links to L02: assessment criterion 2.4

Describe the types of support that people need during change. Remember that the type of support needed will depend on the sort of change which is happening. Give one example of change and list at least two types of support that people may need in order to help them cope with it.

Good communication is especially important during times of change

Benefits of good communication with others

During times of change in the workplace, individuals are understandably more sensitive and unsettled than they would be normally. It is for this reason that good communication throughout the organisation, as well as accurate and timely information, is more important than ever.

Good communication is always necessary in organisations, but it is never more critical then when an organisation is undergoing change. This is because people affected by the change need to have a ready supply of information which should flow from the top of the organisation down through the ranks in a clear and unambiguous manner. The content of the communication should reach all the relevant employees without being changed in any way so that everyone receives the same message.

Employees need to know exactly what is happening, as well as what is expected of them, during times of change, for their peace of mind and happiness. By having a good communication system, many fears and insecurities can be alleviated.

Good communication should also allow for two-way information exchange, so that information can flow back up the organisation too. There should be mechanisms in place whereby employees can air their questions and concerns, maybe using a comments box or by having a nominated manager who will field such queries.

There are several key benefits to good communication:

- All employees receive the same message.
- Information travels both up and down the organisation.

Why do you think reviewing the effects of change is important?

- It is clear and easily understandable.
- Information is given out in good time for people to do what is required of them.
- Everybody is kept informed as to what is happening and what they need to do, so that staff do not feel insecure or uncertain.

> ### ✓ Checklist
>
> Organisations need to ensure that they adopt a good, clear communications strategy. This will make staff feel happier and more secure, which is especially important during times of change.

Visual management techniques

Visual management techniques can be very effective in communicating change to staff. Informative charts and posters can be displayed around the office showing company performance figures, such as sales figures, customer complaints resolved, numbers of calls handled, along with targets for the coming week or month. These enable staff to see, at a glance, the current position along with the target which they must work to.

These techniques can also be used to display artists' impressions of new buildings which are under development, along with office plans for the new premises, enabling staff to see where they will be located once the new premises are completed. This can have a positive effect on morale as it gives staff some certainty as to the future.

Benefits of accurate information during change

The accuracy of information given out in an organisation during times of change is vital because people need to know exactly what is happening on a daily basis, or perhaps more frequently.

If incorrect information is spread around, this could have potentially damaging consequences and may cause further rumours, speculation, scare stories and other unofficial communication channels spreading unhelpful information. All of these things are bad for the organisation and must be avoided at all costs.

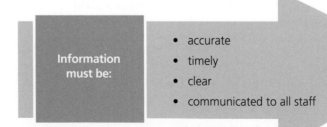

Information must be:
- accurate
- timely
- clear
- communicated to all staff

Figure 227.5: *Accurate information is vital during change*

Portfolio task 227.8

→ Links to LO2: assessment criterion 2.5

Explain the benefits of good communication of accurate information during change. Try to give an example of a change that you have experienced at work. It may be a small change to your working methods, the introduction of a new process or initiative in your department, or it could be a far-reaching change affecting the whole company. Describe how the business communicated information about the change.

Functional Skills

English: Speaking, listening and communication

Portfolio task 227.8 gives you a very good opportunity to generate evidence towards your Functional English Level 2: Speaking, listening and communication. Your assessor may ask you to take part in a discussion about the task, as well as asking you to describe the reasons why good communication is important during times of change. You may also be asked to talk about an example of change which you have experienced at work and to describe how this was communicated. If you have not yet experienced any change, you may wish to talk about how you think it should be communicated.

Your assessor will help you to make sure you gather the correct evidence for your functional skills portfolio.

Identifying the effects of changes on your work

Organisational changes can affect your work in various ways, which may be positive or negative. It is important to be able to identify any resulting effects on your work in order that you can inform your line manager. In this way, any necessary actions can be taken to address your concerns.

These are some of the types of changes you might identify in your work.

Figure 227.6: *Why do you think it is important to identify the effects of change on your work?*

- Inadequate skills. After the introduction of a new system, your skill level or competency in the use of the new system may be lower than you would like. This could be due to a lack of training. Additional training sessions tailored to your individual needs will address this.

- Poor morale. Your morale may be lowered as a result of undergoing a change to your working practices. This may affect your overall work rate and general performance at work, as well as making you unhappy or anxious. If you think your morale has been badly affected, you will need to speak to your line manager.

- Fall in productivity. Your productivity is your overall output per day or per week, and can be evaluated in terms of calls made, letters written, orders processed and emails answered.

- Rise in error rate. If there is a noticeable increase in your error rate, this may indicate a problem with the change in working methods and needs to be addressed by your line manager.

There are several reasons why it is important to check on the effects of change on your work.

- To see whether the change in working methods has produced the desired results or not.
- To identify any other things which need to be done to make improvements or corrections.
- To evaluate whether another working method may be a better approach to the situation.
- To identify any unintended effects of change on your work and to take steps to correct these.

Portfolio task 227.9   ➔   Links to LO2: assessment criterion 2.6

Describe how to identify the effects of changes on your work and give reasons why it is important to do so. It may help you to answer the following questions:

- Have the effects of change on your job been positive or negative?
- Are you now completing your tasks more quickly or more slowly?
- Have you had to learn new technologies?
- Have you had to take on new tasks?

Purpose of reviewing the effects of changes on people

Businesses need to review the effects of implementing new working practices and technologies on the organisation because these require major investment in time and resources and can be very expensive. This expenditure will have to be justified to stakeholders in terms of gains achieved as a result of the change.

How can you measure the effects of change?

A review involves evaluating whether the change which was implemented has had the result which was intended, and could be measured in many ways including:

- increased revenue
- increased productivity
- reduced **wastage**
- reduced **absenteeism**.

It is important for the business to review the effects of change on staff in order to:

- identify any problems with morale and deal with them as quickly as possible
- identify **skills gaps** which may now be apparent and implement training initiatives
- monitor overall staff performance levels and evaluate whether they have met with the planned targets.

Staff morale

Morale may have suffered as a result of the change and it might be necessary to put plans in place to address this. Failure to identify problems with morale can lead to issues for the business in the future such as reduced performance and productivity, which will cost the business in terms of lost output, and staff leaving the organisation, with the expense of recruitment and training to replace them. According to the Chartered Institute of Personnel and Development, the average cost to a business of replacing a member of staff is £4333 (*2007 Recruitment, Retention and Turnover Survey*, CIPD). Ensuring an effective plan is put in place to monitor staff morale will prevent these costly problems and will help the business find ways to keep staff happy in their work.

Skills gaps

Skills gaps are a common problem after a business has implemented a change in the way it operates, such as the introduction of new technology in the factory or office. They can be removed by training and development initiatives to make sure the employee learns the new skills needed as quickly as possible.

Performance

A business must monitor staff performance levels to check whether they meet targets. If not, the business must implement interim **benchmarks** to help staff focus on these. It must also look deeper into any performance issues as this may signify a potential problem with the change which needs to be addressed.

Key terms

Wastage – waste caused by business processes such as manufacturing.

Absenteeism – employee absence from work.

Skills gaps – the difference between the skills an employee has and those required to carry out a job.

Benchmarks – standards set out for minimum performance targets.

✓ Checklist

Benchmarks are not only used in individual organisations. They are widely used to set standards of performance for all businesses in a particular industry.

Purpose of reviewing the effects of changes on processes and outcomes

The effects of change on processes and outcomes must be reviewed in order to:

● identify and measure improvements in productivity – it is these improvements which will justify the organisation's expenditure on the change initiatives

● identify any shortcomings or areas where results have not been as planned and take action to address these – failure to do so will mean the change will not have the desired positive effects on the business.

The process of monitoring and reviewing the effects of change must be a continuous one and not simply a one-off, token activity by management. Monitoring and reviewing are integral to the whole process and are used to feed back into the decision-making process. This way, any problems identified will be dealt with quickly and properly.

Portfolio task 227.10 → Links to LO2: assessment criterion 2.7

Explain the purpose of reviewing the effects of changes on:

● people

● processes and outcomes.

Remember that the effects of changes on people can be either positive or negative. They may also affect the quality of processes and outcomes in a good or bad way. Say why it is important for the business to know about these possible effects.

Describe ways of reviewing the effects of changes on:

● people

● processes and outcomes.

It may help you to look back over the content in the sections above before you begin writing your answer for this portfolio task. Include two ways of reviewing the effects of change on people and two ways of reviewing the effects of change on processes and outcomes in your answer.

Ways of reviewing the effects of changes on people

The main methods for reviewing the effects of change at work on people include:

● one-to-one interviews

● questionnaires

● group discussions

● performance measurement techniques.

One-to-one interviews

The use of one-to-one interviews offers a good way of collecting very detailed information from each individual. It also allows free, unstructured feedback from staff that may shed light on areas which would otherwise be difficult to uncover. The main disadvantage of this method is that it is very time-consuming and the data collected can be difficult to **collate** because each person may respond in a different way. This means it will be difficult to put the information gathered into graphs, charts and reports without a lot of work.

Key term

Collate – to collect together and analyse.

Questionnaires

Questionnaires can be distributed to all staff in order to review the effects of changes on them. These are a good option where a business needs to get data from a large pool of employees, as they are relatively quick to complete. The results are also quite easy to collate and to summarise in a report because a questionnaire is structured and the answers fit into categories. The anonymity can also encourage honesty. The main drawback of this method is that it does not allow for free feedback from staff, so detailed or unstructured information cannot easily be collected using this method.

Group discussions

Holding discussion groups is a potentially valuable method of data gathering. It allows the free flow of detailed information, as with one-to-one interviews. A benefit of group discussions is that they allow people to compare experiences and share their views with each other. Also, the business can collect information from a large number of people at once. Perhaps the main drawback of this approach is that people may be put off contributing to the group if they are the only one who is not getting on well with their job when everyone else seems to be coping with the changes. As a result, they may not speak up and discuss a problem if they feel it will reflect badly on them.

Performance measurement techniques

Taking objective measurements of staff performance is a good indicator of how a change at work has affected employees. Typically, this could involve measuring results such as:

- numbers of calls made
- numbers of complaints resolved
- number of pages typed.

However, one drawback of this method is that it does not explain the results, especially where problems with performance are uncovered. Further investigation would then be necessary in order to get to the root cause of these problems.

Ways of reviewing the effects of changes on processes and outcomes

In order to review the effects of changes on processes and outcomes, businesses look at the figures for things such as:

- error rates
- work flow
- productivity
- complaints.

Key term

Mailshots – marketing letters sent out by a company to people on a mailing list.

Error rates

If you measure the error rates of key processes in the business, such as errors per hundred **mailshots** sent out, or errors per hundred orders processed, this will give you a picture of how well any changes at work have affected key processes. If the changes have resulted in fewer errors being made than before, this is a sign that the change has improved the overall efficiency of a process. Remember, fewer errors mean lower costs for the business!

Productivity

Productivity means the amount of work that people get through. So, the more productive a person is, the more gets done. Obviously, the more that can be done, the better it is for the business. Productivity can refer to any task or process at work, such as the number of the number of invoices sent out or the number of pages typed per minute.

A version of this table, ready for you to complete, is available to download from www.contentextra.com/businessadmin

··

Activity 1

Think of all the different jobs which you do at work and of the different ways in which your own productivity can be measured. Select three jobs or tasks. List them in the table below, and, for each one, list one way in which your productivity is, or could be, measured.

Task	Way in which productivity could be measured
1	

Figure 227.7: *The number of complaints received is a good indicator of the state of current business practice*

Work flow

Work flow describes the stages which a job or process has to go through until it is complete. If work flows can be made quicker or more streamlined, then this is a good thing for the business as it means more can be done in a shorter time. This is a similar idea to productivity.

Complaints

The number of complaints received by the business is a good measure of the effect of a change (see Figure 227.7). If there is a major reduction in the number of complaints received following the change, this is a sign that things have improved. If, on the other hand, complaints are increasing, the business may need to look again at the change and implement an alternative solution or provide further training or support for staff.

Portfolio task 227.11 → Links to LO2: assessment criterion 2.8

Describe ways of reviewing the effects of changes on people, processes and outcomes.

Your role in responding to change

Your individual response to change at work will have an impact on how well you deal with it and how you ultimately move forward in your career. The way in which you choose to behave, whether you embrace the change or are resistant to it, will also affect how well the change works in your department. You will look in more detail at some of these issues in this section.

Purpose of change as part of a process of continuous improvement

Businesses everywhere invest large sums of money in making changes to the way they operate and to the things they make and sell in order to produce more profit, improve the standing of the business, make it more secure and guarantee its future prosperity.

So, you can see that change contributes to improvement. It is also something which needs to be an ongoing process and not a one-off activity. In this way, the business is always actively looking at how it can be more efficient and provide better products and services to its customers.

Kaizen

The idea of change for continuous improvement is closely related to Kaizen, which is a **philosophy** of continuous change for improvement by constantly making small changes covering all areas of a business. Kaizen originated in Japan and has since been adopted by companies all over the world. Its central idea is that if everyone in the business makes small improvements to what they do at work on an ongoing basis, the overall effect will result in a huge improvement to the business. Kaizen needs all employees to participate in it for it to work. It also assumes all employees are equal, so that one person's ideas are as valid as the next person's.

Toyota is well known for using Kaizen. Employees work in teams and use methods such as **quality circles** to suggest ideas for improving the quality of products and processes.

Other ideas which are closely related to Kaizen include:

- total quality management (TQM) – an approach to management which puts quality and the reduction of errors and waste at the heart of every process
- lean production techniques – production methods which use only the minimum resources needed to produce the product
- just-in-time (JIT) supply methods – the business gets the raw materials (stock) it requires at the moment it is ready to use them during the manufacturing process. This reduces the amount of stock lying around the factory. Unused stock costs the business money, so JIT is a good method of keeping down costs.

> **Key terms**
>
> **Philosophy** – a belief or a set of values.
>
> **Quality circles** – groups of workers who meet together to discuss how to make improvements to their working methods to produce better results.

Figure 227.8: *Toyota uses Kaizen methods*

Can you see a common thread to the three ideas explained above? They all involve:

- stripping out waste
- using only what is needed when it is needed
- putting quality at the heart of every process.

One well-known company that uses lean production methods is Tesco. Its strapline, 'Every little helps', is a perfect example of the Kaizen approach.

Portfolio task 227.12 ➔ Links to LO3: assessment criterion 3.1

Explain the purpose of change as part of a process of continuous improvement. In your answer, remember to talk about Kaizen, what it means and the sort of changes involved in the Kaizen approach.

Possible effects of changes on your own values

Once you have experienced a change in the way things are processed or organised at work, you may well find that your own opinions and values have changed too. You may see things differently and this may cause you to rethink previously held ideas.

Certain aspects of work may well become more important to you. Targets may have become more visible and are published monthly, whereas before, nobody really told you specifically what you had to work to. Similarly, if there are new processes in place, such as follow-up calls being made to customers to establish levels of satisfaction, you may suddenly become very aware of the importance of providing excellent customer service to every single caller.

Portfolio task 227.13 ➔ Links to LO3: assessment criterion 3.2

Explain the possible effects of changes at work on your values. Try to include an example of a change which affected your work and say how it changed your opinions on some aspect of your work.

Benefits of responding positively to changes

Change in business may be sudden or gradual. It may be expected or a surprise. It may be something minor or involve a major change in your working life. Whatever form the change at work takes, your response to it is very important. The way in which you react can be positive or negative, and it is quite understandable that you may have certain reservations. However, before you do or say anything, take a moment to think. The reaction you give will have consequences for you and for your reputation as a professional in the workplace. Try to focus on the positive aspects of the change which is happening.

There are many ways in which you can benefit from being positive in your response to changes at work.

Professionalism

This relates to your valued position as a close assistant to your manager. They will be relying on you to be outwardly professional and to be loyal to the company, especially at a challenging time which a period of change can be. Your professionalism can have a huge impact on other members of the department. A positive attitude will filter through to the whole team and will have a beneficial effect on their response to change.

Future career progression

By responding positively to change you will be seen by your peers – and your manager – as a good, dependable role model within the company and as someone who has the potential to progress to a more senior position of responsibility in the future.

Positive thinking

When faced with challenging or uncertain conditions, the way you choose to act is often an important factor in determining the outcome. If you act as if you are doing the job you aspire to in the future, you are more likely to be viewed as someone who is capable of the position, exactly because you are already displaying those behaviours. If you do not aim high in the first place, how will you achieve your career ambitions?

Portfolio task 227.14 → Links to LO3: assessment criterion 3.3

Explain the benefits of responding positively to changes. Use an example of a change which you have experienced at work and show the benefits of responding in a positive manner.

Evidence collection

For the remaining tasks in this unit, you will need to carry out various tasks at work and then produce evidence to show that you have demonstrated the various skills and competences listed below.

Evidence can be collected in a number of different ways. For example, it can be either a signed witness testimony from a colleague or line manager, a copy of any related emails or letters you have produced, or a verbal discussion with your assessor.

Speak to your assessor to identify the best methods to use in order to complete each task and remember to keep copies of all the evidence which you produce.

Responding to change

Portfolio task 227.15 → Links to LO4: assessment criteria 4.1, 4.2, 4.3, 4.4, 4.5, 4.6 and 4.7

Gather evidence of your work to show your assessor that you have successfully carried out the tasks outlined in the table below. Check with your assessor on the best ways of gathering evidence for each of the tasks before you begin.

Task	Evidence collected
4.1 Identify changes needed in your own area of work	
4.2 Make suggestions for change	
4.3 Complete your own work tasks using changed procedures or ways of working	
4.4 Identify where training or other support is needed	
4.5 Actively seek support, as required	
4.6 Give support to other people during change, or seek support, as required	
4.7 Ask questions to clarify issues	

A version of this table, ready for you to complete, is available to download from www.contentextra.com/businessadmin

Supporting the evaluation of change

Portfolio task 227.16 → Links to LO5: assessment criteria 5.1, 5.2

Gather evidence of your work to show your assessor that you have successfully carried out the tasks outlined in the table below. Check with your assessor on the best ways of gathering evidence for each of the tasks before you begin.

Task	Evidence collected
5.1 Give feedback on the effects of changes in your own work	
5.2 Make suggestions for further actions, as required	

A version of this table, ready for you to complete, is available to download from www.contentextra.com/businessadmin

Check your knowledge

1 Which of the following are possible external triggers for change in an organisation?

a. An office move for the accounts department.

b. An increase in profit.

c. A reduction in office gossip.

d. A change in the market which affects the demand for the company's products.

2 Which of the following is *not* an internal trigger for change in an organisation?

a. A need to cut costs in certain areas of the business.

b. A need to reduce staffing numbers.

c. A change around in the organisation of internal functions.

d. A change of government.

3 Look at the following statements about the effects of change on people. Which one do you agree with most?

a. Change is always a bad thing for people.

b. Change is only ever external.

c. Change can affect people both positively and negatively.

d. Change only happens when you plan it yourself.

4 Sometimes, as a result of change, a business needs to make a member of staff redundant. What does redundant mean?

a. A person's job no longer exists.

b. The business no longer exists.

c. The person has to move to another area of the country.

d. The person has to go to a competitor.

5 How can change benefit an organisation?

a. Cutting profit.

b. Causing external triggers.

c. Removing inefficiencies and streamlining processes.

d. Removing old paper files.

6 How can individuals support changes which are happening at work?

a. Make up their own rules for running the new office processes.

b. Work late to catch up on unfinished jobs.

c. Maintain a positive approach to new processes with work colleagues and managers.

d. Ignore new rules.

7 Why should all staff be involved in discussions about change?

a. To keep them in the dark.

b. To allow them to input their ideas and participate in the process.

c. To stop staff resigning.

d. To save money.

8 Which of the following will *not* help you prepare for a move to a new office?

a. Going on a visit to the new office to see where you will be sitting and what new furniture you may need.

b. Introducing yourself to your new colleagues before you move.

c. Taking the week of the move off to avoid the issue.

d. Packing up your office things and labelling the boxes neatly ready for the removals firm to move them.

9 One of the possible negative effects of change on people is low morale. What does low morale mean?

a. Low wage rises.

b. Staff are generally unhappy at work.

c. Staff are badly behaved.

d. Bonuses are low.

10 What is a skills gap?

a. The gap between the older and younger workers.

b. A gap which the company made by not responding to change.

c. The gap between the skills which an employee currently has and the skills which are needed as a result of change.

d. The gap between managers and staff.

Answers to these questions can be found at www.contentextra.com/businessadmin

What your assessor is looking for

Each unit in this qualification comprises two types of assessment requirements. These are:

- knowledge-based learning outcomes
- performance indicators.

In order to prepare for and succeed in completing this unit, your assessor will require you to be able to demonstrate competence in all of the performance criteria listed in the table below.

Your assessor will guide you through the assessment process, but it is likely that for this unit you will need to:

- complete short written narratives or personal statements explaining your answers
- take part in professional discussions with your assessor to explain your answers verbally

- complete observations with your assessor ensuring that they can observe you carrying out your work tasks
- produce any relevant work products to help demonstrate how you have completed the assessment criteria
- ask your manager, a colleague or a customer for witness testimonies explaining how you have completed the assessment criteria.

The evidence which you generate for the assessment criteria in this unit may also count towards your evidence collection for some of the other units in this qualification. Your assessor will provide support and guidance on this.

The table below outlines the portfolio tasks which you need to complete for this unit, mapped to their associated assessment criteria.

The table below outlines the portfolio tasks which you need to complete for this unit, mapped to their associated assessment criteria.

Task and page reference	Mapping assessment criteria
Portfolio task 227.1 (page 147)	Assessment criterion: 1.1
Portfolio task 227.2 (page 148)	Assessment criterion: 1.2
Portfolio task 227.3 (page 152)	Assessment criterion: 1.3
Portfolio task 227.4 (page 153)	Assessment criterion: 2.1
Portfolio task 227.5 (page 155)	Assessment criterion: 2.2
Portfolio task 227.6 (page 156)	Assessment criterion: 2.3
Portfolio task 227.7 (page 156)	Assessment criterion: 2.4
Portfolio task 227.8 (page 159)	Assessment criterion: 2.5
Portfolio task 227.9 (page 160)	Assessment criterion: 2.6
Portfolio task 227.10 (page 162)	Assessment criterion: 2.7
Portfolio task 227.11 (page 164)	Assessment criterion: 2.8
Portfolio task 227.12 (page 166)	Assessment criterion: 3.1
Portfolio task 227.13 (page 166)	Assessment criterion: 3.2
Portfolio task 227.14 (page 167)	Assessment criterion: 3.3
Portfolio task 227.15 (page 168)	Assessment criteria: 4.1, 4.2, 4.3, 4.4, 4.5, 4.6, 4.7
Portfolio task 227.16 (page 168)	Assessment criteria: 5.1, 5.2

Unit Q212

Produce documents in a business environment

What you will learn

- Understand the purpose of producing high-quality and attractive documents in a business environment
- Know the resources and technology available and how to use them when producing documents in a business environment
- Understand the purpose of following procedures when producing documents in a business environment
- Be able to prepare for tasks
- Be able to produce documents to agreed specifications

Introduction

In this unit, you will learn about the different types of documents that are produced during the course of normal business activities. You will also understand the necessity of using the correct computer programs and layout tools to create high-quality, well laid-out and well-presented business documents that meet the required deadlines, and explore how to store these documents safely so that any confidentiality is safeguarded.

The types of documents that you might investigate are reports, invoices, purchase orders, memos, presentations, spreadsheets and marketing publications such as posters, flyers and leaflets. Whatever industry or field of work you are in, there is always a need to create such documents, and present them to the target audience in a way that maintains the corporate identity of the company.

Working in an office means that you come across documents regularly, and realising the relative importance of each is a skill that you need to develop. Just knowing where the important information on a memo is, for example, means that when you receive one, you will be able to identify quickly how much time you have to complete the task, and when the deadline is. Additionally, if you are sending a memo or email to your colleagues, you will need to know how to set one out so that it is easy for people to read and understand, while not being too time-consuming for you to write. In the case of deadlines, it is important to appreciate that purchase orders must be raised before invoices are received, and the two documents must then match. These are useful skills to learn and facts to know as you develop your working practices.

The purpose of producing high-quality and attractive documents in a business environment

Different types and styles of document

Figure 212.1 shows the many different business documents that are used to communicate with both internal and external **stakeholders**.

Key term

Stakeholders – any individual or organisation that has an interest in the activities of the company you work for.

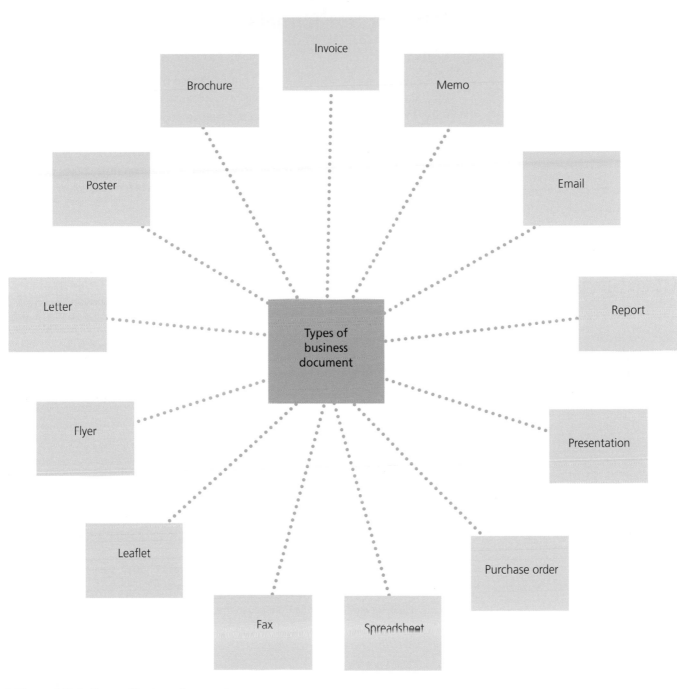

Figure 212.1: *Types of business document*

Different text formats

Letter

While letters are considered to be an old-fashioned method of communication, they are still regularly used within business because they are simple, quick and easy. More importantly, they are also a reference point because they act as a formal written record of what has been said and/or agreed by each party. This means that if there is a dispute or disagreement between your company and another, it is usually straightforward to work out a resolution (this shows how important it is to ensure that any letters you write are detailed and clear). Figure 212.2 shows an example business letter.

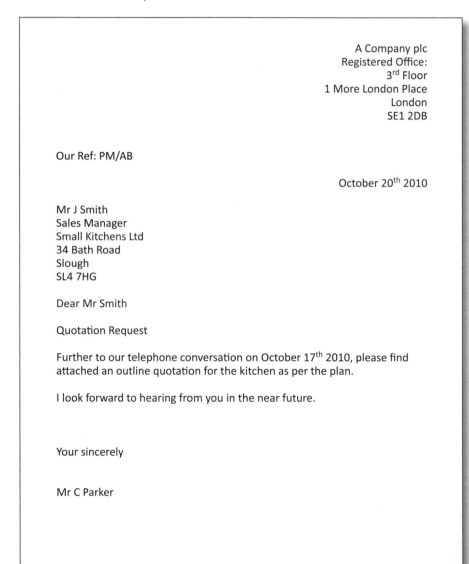

A Company plc
Registered Office:
3rd Floor
1 More London Place
London
SE1 2DB

Our Ref: PM/AB

October 20th 2010

Mr J Smith
Sales Manager
Small Kitchens Ltd
34 Bath Road
Slough
SL4 7HG

Dear Mr Smith

Quotation Request

Further to our telephone conversation on October 17th 2010, please find attached an outline quotation for the kitchen as per the plan.

I look forward to hearing from you in the near future.

Your sincerely

Mr C Parker

Figure 212.2: *Example of a business letter*

Email

Emails (electronic mail) are increasingly replacing letters and faxes (see below) as a formal method of communication in business. Emails are often sent internally – to different members of the same organisation – or externally – to people outside of the organisation. They can be used for a range of purposes – from keeping in touch with colleagues all the way through to negotiating contracts for work.

Communicating by email has become quicker and easier, as many business people now have email access not only on their computers but also through their Blackberry®, iPhone® or similar mobile device. They will often respond at all times of the day and night. Email communication also means that if you are in touch with people all over the world, you can still keep in contact with them while you are in the office.

An email carries the same importance as a letter. Do you always check what you have written before hitting Send?

> ### ✓ Checklist
>
> The important thing to remember about email is that it now carries the same level of importance as writing a letter. You must therefore ensure that anything you write into an email is checked thoroughly, is truthful, and reflects the views of your company.

Memo

A memo (memorandum) is normally sent internally and is used for short, formal messages. It has To/From/Subject/Date fields at the top of the page, followed by the message, and will generally not be signed at the bottom unless the memo is authorising a payment. Nowadays, memos are usually sent by email.

Fax

A fax (facsimile – from Latin meaning an exact copy) is a document that is sent to a recipient using a fax machine and a telephone line. The paper document is prepared, and a fax cover page is included on top. This will give information about:

- today's date
- the number of pages that are being sent
- who is sending the fax
- who the fax is intended for
- a message from the sender to the receiver.

Faxes are sent from business to business where a document is required quickly. Nowadays, however, an email attachment is just as quick (and often cheaper and easier because most documents are typed) so faxes are being used less and less.

AA Accounts plc
Registered Office:
3rd Floor
1 More London Place
London
SE1 2DB

Invoice Reference: PM/AB-Inv1

October 20th 2010

Small Kitchens Ltd
Slough

Order Number: 122

Quantity	Reference	Description	Unit Price £	Total Price £
1	Tel 1	Tele conference	80	80
2	Mtg 1	On-site meeting	190	380
11	Calc 1	VAT and Tax Calculations	150	1650
				2110

Less Discount (3.5%)	73.85
Total (exc VAT)	2036.15
Add VAT @ 20%	
Total Due	407.23
	2443.38

Terms: 60 days from invoice date

VAT Registration Number: 113 000298

Figure 212.3: *Example of an invoice*

Invoice

An invoice is a formal request for payment. An example is shown in Figure 212.3. If you order a mobile phone from a website, for example, the Internet company will send you an email telling you exactly how much you need to pay, including postage and packaging, gift-wrapping and so on. This is an invoice because it confirms exactly what you have ordered and how much you have agreed to pay for the goods.

Often, businesses buy goods on **trade credit**. An invoice will make clear exactly when payment for the goods will be due.

Invoices must be kept by businesses for six years. This is just in case there is a dispute between supplier, business or customer — they act as a record of a contract.

Key term

Trade credit – A system for payment when a business takes the goods, and then pays for them at a later-agreed date (Buy now, pay later).

Purchase order

A purchase order is usually an internal document which you might send to your accounts department. It will detail the items that you wish the department to buy on your behalf, using company funds.

The accounts department will then ensure that money for the items that you have ordered is taken from the correct budget allocation. Often, it will also deal with any discrepancies between what was ordered, and what you have received if there is a problem.

The most important element of the purchase order, from the company's point of view, is the reference number – this means the order that is placed can be tracked from the start, right through to when payment is made for the products.

Leaflet

A leaflet is a type of promotional material usually used by businesses to advertise a special offer, product or event. It is generally A5 in size, contains details of the offer/product/event and is brightly coloured to try to attract as much attention as possible. The leaflet will also include information on how to contact the company and may even have coupons or discount vouchers to try to get more business. Common examples which are likely to come through your letterbox at home are leaflets from delivery pizza companies or from local takeaways (think about what they look like).

Report

A report is another formal business document which tends to be quite long. Generally, you are asked to write a report about a particular topic. You are expected to go away and carry out research, find out thoughts and opinions from others, and then present all your research along with recommendations for how the company should move forward. The structure of a report depends on the type of company you work for, and the task you are set, but it will generally include these sections:

- Aims (what you have been asked to do)
- Purpose (why you are carrying out the task)
- Methodology (how you are going to carry out your research)
- Research (your findings, with graphs, charts, and extracts from text)
- Recommendations and Evaluation (based on your research findings, what action you recommend the company should take).

You should always use headings in a report, and ensure that the cover page includes the title of the report, date, your name, and the corporate livery.

Poster

A poster is another type of promotional material. It differs from a leaflet in that it is designed simply to draw the eye to the basic information that is on it. A poster might be placed in a shop window, bus shelter, noticeboard, or even turned into a billboard advert. It must be eye-catching, bright, colourful and provide outline information so that a potential customer knows where the event/product is, and what they might expect from it.

Flow chart

A flow chart is a logic diagram that shows a process that you could go through, with all the steps involved, and the decisions that you could take along the way (see Figure 212.4). An oval node represents the start or end of a chart, rectangular boxes indicate instructions and diamond shapes contain questions or decisions that you must take.

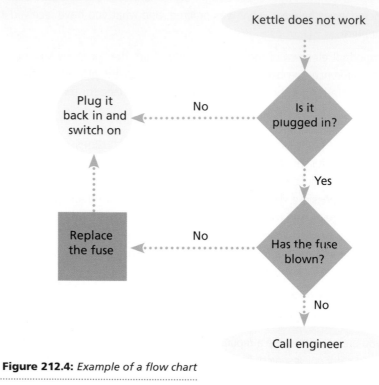

Figure 212.4: *Example of a flow chart*

Spreadsheet

A spreadsheet is usually a numerical document created on a computer that is used to produce accounts, sales forecasts, sales charts and graphs, questionnaire analysis and other similar documents that involve calculations. It is a powerful tool which you can program to complete tasks for you automatically such as calculating sums, averages and drawing.

Companies often set up spreadsheet models so that you could, for example, put details of your pay in each month, and it would tell you how much tax you should be paying, how much your pension contributions should be each month and so on. You may be asked to construct a spreadsheet model as part of your work.

Purpose and benefits of producing high-quality and attractive documents

Whatever document you are trying to create, it is important to follow some basic principles to ensure that the organisation's corporate image is maintained and that the document has a professional and consistent look.

Activity 1

Collect a range of different documents that your organisation produces. Try to obtain examples of the documents shown in Figure 212.1 so that you can appreciate the content and purpose of them as you work through this unit.

Structure

Every document, whether a letter, invoice or even a quick email, will have its own structure and purpose. This enables the person creating it to understand how it should be set out and the recipient to know who the document is from, and what they are expected to do with it.

A business letter should be laid out in a professional manner and printed on corporate **headed paper** before being sent out. Its structure needs to be clear so that the person receiving the letter can understand what you are telling them, and will therefore be able to respond quickly and efficiently.

Business letters are usually divided into three parts.

- Introduction – explain why you are writing to the person and outline what topic/transaction/account the letter is referring to.

- Main content – this part of the letter should explain the details and message that you want to communicate to the recipient. Remember to use a new paragraph for each separate point that you make.

- Conclusion – at the end of the letter remember that it is important to explain either what you are going to do next, or what you are expecting the recipient to do next. Keep this part short and concise – you could use bullet points if appropriate to draw attention to each action required.

Style (tone and corporate)

When constructing any business document, you must remember that you are representing the company that you work for, and not yourself. This means that the language you use when writing must be formal, and not read like you are talking to your friend.

The best business letters have short, punchy sentences which are easy to read and not too complicated. They also use correct punctuation and have been through a spell-checker to correct any mistakes that have been made.

Using formal language means that you must not write a document in the same way as you 'talk' to your friends on social networking sites or by text message. You must use standard English. It is a good idea to ask a colleague you trust to have a look at your final document before submitting it to your manager just in case there are any errors that you have missed.

Content – make a plan

The first thing to do before writing any document is to plan exactly what you are going to include in each section. This way, you can keep to the point you intended to make in each paragraph or section, and the document will be easier to read.

> **Key term**
>
> **Headed paper –** paper that has the company's logo and contact details printed at the top.

Key term

Draft – an early version of a document that is still in the process of being checked for accuracy.

Once you have produced your plan, the next stage is to write a **draft** of your document. Sometimes you will put together more than two drafts before you are happy to submit the final version. It is important to build in time not only to proofread and check the document for spelling, punctuation, grammar and accuracy, but also for a friend or colleague to do this for you too.

The best way of making sure that you have not made grammatical errors is to read the document out loud to yourself. This way, if you have forgotten to put in commas, full-stops and so on, then you will find these quickly and easily.

Portfolio task 212.1

→ Links to LO1: assessment criteria 1.1 (task 1), 1.2 (task 1) and 1.3 (task 2)

1   Select three different types of document that you either send or receive regularly within the context of your job. Explain how each is created and why the company chooses to present them in that way. If you think that any of the documents would be better presented in a different way, explain how and why.

2   Explain the purpose and benefits of producing high-quality and attractive documents.

To help you complete this task, you will need to cover the following points:

a) Why does your company produce the documents that you have identified?

b) Why is it important for your company to ensure that the documents are both attractive to look at, printed on high-quality paper, in colour, designed well, fit for purpose?

Resources and technology – how to use them when producing documents in a business environment

While there are many methods of producing the various business documents that you investigated above, the most common methods are to utilise information and computer technology. The design of logos and other artwork is often outsourced by companies as they do not always have the in-house services of a graphic designer. There are different ways that the content could be entered into the documents, and you will look at some of these methods in this section.

Types of resources available for producing high-quality and attractive documents

Do it yourself!

This is by far the easiest way. Rather than spending a lot of time explaining to someone else how you would like them to create a particular document, it is often better just to do it yourself. You need to feel confident that you have the skills required to create the first draft at least, and then you can always ask colleagues for their support to help refine it to the final version.

Remember to plan what you need to include in the document before you start putting it together. It is also a good idea to collect together images, pictures, photographs before you start, if all possible.

Nowadays, business documents are usually produced electronically, so you will need to use a computer or other appropriate electronic method.

Administration and design support

You may be able to ask your colleagues in administration and/or design to produce your document for you. First, you will need to put together the content of the document such as a letter, report or flow chart.

The admin team may be able to ensure that the document reflects the corporate image, for example company logos are in the correct place on each page, the font styles and sizes are in the corporate style and so on. They may even be able to spell-check the document for you.

The design (marketing) team may be able to provide artwork that you need or would like to include in the document you are producing. This might simply be the company logo or, if you are designing a report with a proposal for some new office layout designs, for example, they may be able to support you in refining the final look of the designs.

Overall, it is important to try to find out where your colleagues' skills lie, so that you can support each other in the production of the document.

The Internet

The Internet contains a vast amount of information. You can always use websites for researching information, finding images and contacting other companies. However, it is important to be selective and check the information you find to make sure that it is credible and reliable. More importantly, if you use images or text that you have found on the Internet, you must check whether it is subject to a copyright constraint. This might mean that you have to pay a royalty to the company for the privilege of using it. If you do not gain permission before using the material, the copyright holder could start legal proceedings.

Reprographic support

Reprographics is simply photocopying but on a large scale. Large organisations usually have a team of people who are responsible for producing multiple copies of documents that staff have created. Therefore, if you are launching a leaflet or poster campaign or need several copies of a large report printed and bound so that they all look professional, you may need to enlist the services of the reprographics team.

Ways of using different resources to produce documents

By hand

While some professionals still work with their hands, in an office situation, most of your work will be completed on a computer. The easiest way of planning what you are going to include in a final document might actually be to scribble some ideas on a piece of paper, and then put it all together on the computer. Some design work could also be done on paper.

Convention now is for everything produced by companies to be compliant with computers, therefore it is best to focus on that!

Using a computer/computer-based device

First, you will need to decide which computer program is likely to be the most appropriate one to use to create your document. For example, if you are writing a letter, then a word-processing program would probably be best; however, if you wanted to create a leaflet or poster, then a desktop publishing program would be more suitable.

Once you have chosen the program, you will need to make sure that you have all the correct information and non-text files (images, diagrams, photos and so on) to hand before starting to create your document. Then you should follow the plan you have created to produce the document. Ensure that you check it thoroughly for errors before submitting the final version. Remember also to save it regularly in a suitable folder, with a filename you are likely to recognise.

Types of technology available for inputting, formatting and editing text

Computer keyboard and mouse

Typing information into a computer using a keyboard and mouse will probably be the way that you produce most of your documents. A mouse is a versatile tool which will help you to rearrange designs, quickly resize objects and tables and highlight text so that formatting changes can be made easily.

What input devices do you use? Are there any other devices that you would find useful?

Digital drawing tablet

If you work in a media/graphic design/creative environment, you are likely to work with a digital drawing tablet. This can be used to construct images and logos which could be included in a document that you wish to create. Use of this tool often requires specialist training, so make sure that you are familiar with it before trying it out.

Digital media devices

These include still cameras, video cameras and sound recorders. They will provide a multimedia dimension to your document and could help to make it more attractive for the recipient to look at.

Key term

Multinational – a company that operates in more than one country.

Language support and voice control

If the company that you work for is a **multinational**, you may be required to produce your documents in more than one language. For this, the formatting and checking may need to be completed in a language other than English. There are various translator packages available, so you may need to check whether your company has one, and whether you will be required to use it.

For those people who suffer from repetitive strain injury (RSI), for example, and therefore find it more difficult to type for long periods, voice control software will enable them to talk into their computer which will automatically input their words on to the screen.

Portfolio task 212.2
→ Links to LO2: assessment criteria 2.1, 2.2 and 2.3

Create a PowerPoint® presentation to demonstrate the corporate identity of the organisation you work for. Your presentation will need to address the following areas:

- Describe the types of resources available to you for creating the high-quality and attractive documents that you regularly produce.

- Outline the different ways you could use these resources to produce the documents.

- Describe the main features of at least two different types of technology available for inputting, formatting and editing the text that goes into the documents referred to above.

The presentation should be aimed at colleagues who are at a similar level of seniority in the company to you. It should be imaginative and contain images or other media.

Office life

Vinny's story

My name is Vinny Carlotti, I'm 19 and work for a well-known marketing agency in London. One Monday morning, I was given an assignment to produce a glossy magazine cover design for a large department store. My manager told me that it had to look modern, and the focus should be a games console of my choice. To accompany the design, she asked me to write a formal letter to the managing director of the store with a full explanation of my ideas.

I spent the whole of Tuesday morning researching possible ideas for the design, and in the afternoon worked on the design of the front cover staying at the office until I had finished it at around 7 p.m. On Wednesday I was back in the office at 8 a.m. and wrote the letter to the managing director before leaving for a meeting at lunchtime. On Wednesday afternoon, I emailed the design and letter to the managing director of the department store.

First thing on Friday morning, I was called into a meeting with my manager who was very angry. The managing director had phoned her to say that while my design was acceptable (though not refined), the quality of the letter I had sent was 'appalling'.

Ask the expert

Q How should I handle a similar situation?

A In future, it's a good idea to adopt a policy of 'less haste, more speed'. Take more time to clarify the purpose of the task in hand, and then ensure that you check the outcomes carefully with your manager before sending anything to clients. You could also ask a trusted colleague to proofread important letters before you submit them to your manager for sign off.

Top tips

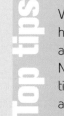

Vinny's major mistake was to become overexcited about the task. He rushed his research and the design stage and did not ask any of his colleagues, let alone his manager, for feedback before sending off the letter and design. Normally, a designer would produce several different designs over a period of time, and then some consultation would take place before changes were made and the final design agreed ready to send to the client. The accompanying letter would be signed off by the manager prior to it being sent.

The purpose of following procedures when producing documents in a business environment

The benefits of agreeing purpose, content, style and deadlines

Agreeing these points before starting to produce the documents means that you will have less work to do to refine them after the initial draft stage.

Purpose of document

Agreeing the purpose of a document with your manager or another colleague is important as the purpose will often determine who the audience is. This will change how you write and the way that you lay out the document. It will also affect the language that you use. For example, if you were designing a leaflet to customers advertising a new component that your factory has devised, it would be very different to a poster advertising the annual staff summer picnic.

Content and style

The content of your documents will very much depend on the purpose and audience. The style of writing, and the level of detail that you include, will be at a higher level for senior managers, and possibly more persuasive if aimed at customers.

The style of your documents should always reflect the corporate ethos of your company. The colour scheme, strapline, logo and font styles should use the corporate style so that it is easily identifiable.

Deadlines

Agreeing deadlines with your manager is essential, as they will undoubtedly want to check whatever you produce before it is distributed more widely. They may well want to agree an internal deadline of at least a week before the final proof is due so that there is enough time to check and correct any errors.

Different ways of organising content needed for documents

There are many ways of setting out documents. The most appropriate methods depend on what the purpose of the document is and who the audience might be.

Tables

Tables may be used to present information, especially if your aim is to compare different factors or to show different stages in a process. They are useful to provide a break between extended pieces of text.

Text

Text is useful for providing explanations and to put situations into context. However, sometimes there may be text 'overkill'. This means that there is too much text in a document and because of a lack of images or tables or another feature to break up the words, the reader can easily lose their place.

Images

Images, such as photos, pictures, drawings, cartoons, graphs and charts, can help to put the text into context. They also help to provide some contrast on the page and give the reader something else to look at.

Columns

Newspapers and magazines use columns to try to fit more text on a page. It is another valid tool for presenting information, and if the situation allows for it, and you feel it appropriate, then use the format.

Organisation

There is no 'best way' of organising content on a page. The only way of determining the most appropriate way to do this is to look at the purpose of the document, take into account the audience, and discuss the plans you have with your manager before going ahead, especially if you have a radical plan.

Activity 2

Look at well-known publications for ideas and try to identify what is 'good' or what you like about them. This activity will help you to start to generate ideas about how you could make your mark on a document's layout.

Checking the finished documents for accuracy and correctness

Spelling, punctuation and grammar

Most word-processing packages have a built-in spelling and grammar checker. It is important to make use of these before you proofread the document yourself. Once you have used the electronic checker, then you must also manually check through the document before submitting it for review.

Technical terms

If you are not yet comfortable with your own use of technical terminology and context, then it is a good idea to ask a colleague to proofread the document for you and to provide feedback.

Readability

Once you have checked your second draft through thoroughly, do a final check by reading the entire document out loud to yourself. This will enable you to spot any final punctuation errors which you should correct before submitting the draft to your manager. The document must read clearly and flow from one paragraph or section to the next. If you are still unsure of what to do, or you are unhappy with the document, then ask a colleague for some support.

The purpose of storing documents safely and securely and storage methods

Secure storage

There are several methods used to store document securely.

Computer

When you save documents on your computer, or on the network at the office, you must ensure that if they contain anything confidential that the file should be password-protected. Only the people who 'need to know' should have access to the password.

You should also make a back-up of important documents so that you have a spare copy should the original get corrupted in any way.

Filing cabinet

If you wish to keep paper copies of documents, then it is important to file them sensibly, and in accordance with company procedures, so as to make sure that they can be found if required. The size of the cabinet also needs to be suitable for the size of the document to be stored.

Where the content is confidential, the filing cabinet should have a lock, with only a small number of people authorised to have access to it.

A 'need-to-know basis'

If you are working on commercially sensitive material, you may be working on a 'need-to-know basis'. This means that only the people who are involved with the project 'need to know' what is happening. This might also mean that if you are preparing some accounts or a series of confidential invoices to be sent out, you might be one of the only people who knows what is in the invoice. This level of trust that your company puts in you means that you must not share any information with other colleagues unless they 'need to know'.

Do you have access to storage facilities suitable for the items you need to store?

Confidentiality and data protection

Many commercial practices are subject to confidentiality clauses to preserve the working relationship that the companies involved have. It is therefore vital to make sure that any information that is shared with you about a contract, for example, is only shared on the documents that you produce if you are expressly asked to, or indeed you are clear that it is necessary.

The Data Protection Act 1998 means that companies are bound to make sure that any personal data that they hold about individuals is held securely, cannot be accessed by anyone who does not have a legitimate reason for seeking it and is not shared with any other parties. This might mean that if you are preparing a mailshot, you would need to check whether any of your customers have asked not to be contacted by you or a third party.

Meeting deadlines

As mentioned earlier, it is not only important to agree deadlines but also to meet them. From a personal perspective, it shows that you are a professional and can be trusted. From a corporate perspective, it portrays a good impression of the company. You will build and develop a reputation for being reliable if you regularly meet the deadlines that you are set or agree to, and therefore it is in your interests to do so.

Portfolio task 212.3

→ Links to LO1: assessment criteria 1.1 (task 1), 1.2 (task 1) and 1.3 (task 2)

The assessment criteria for this learning outcome tie in closely to learning outcomes 4 and 5. You can therefore choose how you are assessed for learning outcome 3. You can *either*:

- create an advice leaflet which covers the areas outlined below

or

- while completing the portfolio tasks for learning outcome 5, annotate the documents that you create to explain the areas outlined below (that is, what have you done while creating the documents).

Areas to be covered (in the advice leaflet *or* your annotated documents):

- Explain the benefits of agreeing the purpose, content, style and deadlines for producing documents.

- Outline different ways of organising content needed for documents, which includes layouts for text and non-text items.

- Describe ways of checking the finished documents for accuracy (spelling, punctuation, grammar, correctness), and why you need to check the finished document.

- Explain the purpose of storing documents safely and securely, and ways in which you can do so.

- Explain the purpose of confidentiality and data protection when preparing documents.

- Explain the purpose and benefits of meeting deadlines.

Prepare for tasks

This section requires you to provide evidence that you can effectively prepare for the creation of business documents. This means that you will need to demonstrate that you have understood what you have learned in the first three learning outcomes of this unit and collect information in an organised fashion. You will then use this information to address learning outcome 5 and actually create the documents.

Prior to creating the documents, you will need to know:

- what they are to contain
- their purpose
- which department they are coming from and going to
- the style and deadline
- other internal information that will be specific to your organisation, such as reference numbers.

The guidelines given portfolio task 212.4 are in outline only — you must ensure that all details that would be included in the documents you are going to create should be on the pro forma.

Portfolio task 212.4   ➡ Links to LO4: assessment criterion 4.1

Create a pro forma that you and your colleagues could use before putting together your next set of business documents.

The pro forma should contain space to include detail about:

- the purpose of the document
- its content
- the style it should be written and presented in (including some appreciation of who the audience will be, and whether the document is to be sent internally or externally)
- the deadline by which the document should be completed.

You can decide whether to create a simple pro forma, or whether to include predetermined categories for some of the areas. You will need to use the pro forma when you carry out portfolio task 212.5, so make sure it is going to be of help to you!

Produce documents to agreed specifications

This section will enable you to bring together everything that you have learned in this unit. You will need to refer specifically to the content and theory from learning outcome 3 and the preparation that you completed for learning outcome 4 so that you can produce the documents that you have been asked to by your manager.

Evidence collection

To successfully complete this learning outcome, you will need to provide evidence that you have learned and understood the content within this unit and can successfully go through the process of preparing, organising and producing the documents that you are required to, and to the required standard.

You must produce at least *three* different documents that would be in the normal duties of your job.

For each task below, you will need to ensure that you keep evidence of the documents you create, at each stage of their production. For example, you would need to save the original file, explain the processes you went through to check it for accuracy, and then print out the revised document after the changes are made.

Unit Q212 Produce documents in a business environment

Portfolio task 212.5

→ Links to LO5: assessment criteria 5.1, 5.2, 5.3, 5.4, 5.5, 5.6, 5.7, 5.8, 5.9 and 5.10

1 Ensure that all your resources (technological, physical, human) are in place ready for you to start creating your documents. You may be able to provide evidence of this through emails which arrange for colleagues to help you with language support, for example, or to complete some design work.

2 Collect together all the text, images, data, graphs and charts that you are going to include in your documents. It would be useful to organise these carefully in folders on your computer so you can access what you need quickly and easily when you need it.

3 If appropriate, ensure that you use technology to help produce your documents. This could be as simple as typing a letter on the computer or doing some design work using a drawing tablet. If you are going to use technology to complete some of the task, then make sure you use the most appropriate program.

4 It is now time to create your documents. Remember to format and produce them to the agreed style, ensuring they are designed using your company's corporate identity.

5 If required, include any 'non-text objects' such as images, tables and spreadsheets in appropriate places within your documents.

6 Now that the first drafts of your documents are complete, you must record how you have checked them for accuracy (spelling, punctuation, grammar, suitable words).

7 Make any changes that you need to so that the documents are perfect and ready for distribution.

8 Check again with your manager that you have produced the correct documents to the standards required, and within the timescales originally set out.

9 Ensure that copies of the documents you have created are filed away safely, and with passwords and/or in secure filing cabinets (if required). If any of your colleagues need to be made aware of the passwords and/or locations of the documents, then make sure that you communicate this to them.

10 The documents that you have created are now ready for presentation/distribution, so that is your final job!

Check your knowledge

1 List four different documents that you might produce in the normal course of your work.

2 What is it important to do when writing a formal business document?

   a. Use slang language.

   b. Write formally using high-quality language.

   c. Remember that you are representing the company you work for.

   d. Write in MSN language.

3 Identify three appropriate methods of checking that a finished document is complete and accurate.

   a. Send it to the client.

   b. Ask a colleague to read it.

   c. Use the spell-checker on the computer.

   d. Read it out loud to yourself.

   e. Do not bother checking it and assume it is perfect first time.

4 Identify two methods of ensuring security of confidential documents.

   a. Lock them in a secure filing cabinet.

   b. Print the document and leave it on your desk.

   c. Password-protect the file on the computer.

   d. Ensure that all your colleagues know the content of the document.

5 Identify two acceptable ways of producing high-quality documents.

   a. Never ask for help even if you are struggling.

   b. Try to organise for a designer to complete the artwork if that is not your strength.

   c. Mis-spell the name of the star performer for a gala evening.

   d. Ensure the final document is proof-checked before it goes to print.

Answers to these questions can be found at www.contentsextra.com/businessadmin

What your assessor is looking for

Each unit in this qualification comprises two types of assessment requirements. These are:

- knowledge-based learning outcomes
- performance indicators.

In order to prepare for and succeed in completing this unit, your assessor will require you to be able to demonstrate competence in all of the performance criteria listed in the table below.

Your assessor will guide you through the assessment process, but it is likely that for this unit you will need to:

- complete short written narratives or personal statements explaining your answers
- take part in professional discussions with your assessor to explain your answers verbally

- complete observations with your assessor ensuring that they can observe you carrying out your work tasks
- produce any relevant work products to help demonstrate how you have completed the assessment criteria
- ask your manager, a colleague or a customer for witness testimonies explaining how you have completed the assessment criteria.

The evidence which you generate for the assessment criteria in this unit may also count towards your evidence collection for some of the other units in this qualification. Your assessor will provide support and guidance on this.

The table below outlines the portfolio tasks which you need to complete for this unit, mapped to their associated assessment criteria.

Task and page reference	Mapping assessment criteria
Portfolio task 212.1 (page 180)	Assessment criteria: 1.1 (task 1), 1.2 (task 1), 1.3 (task 2)
Portfolio task 212.2 (page 184)	Assessment criteria: 2.1, 2.2, 2.3
Portfolio task 212.3 (page 190)	Assessment criteria: 1.1 (task 1), 1.2 (task 1), 1.3 (task 2)
Portfolio task 212.4 (page 191)	Assessment criterion: 4.1
Portfolio task 212.5 (page 192)	Assessment criteria: 5.1, 5.2, 5.3, 5.4, 5.5, 5.6, 5.7, 5.8, 5.9, 5.10

Unit Q213

Produce text from notes

What you will learn

- Understand preparing text from notes
- Understand the purpose and benefits of following procedures when preparing text from notes
- Be able to prepare for text from notes
- Be able to prepare text from notes

Introduction

The administrator's role is to provide support to the employees in an organisation. This includes drafting and producing all types of documents for internal and/or external use either from notes, audio or shorthand. It is usual for these documents to follow a certain format based on the organisation's house style or standard commercial layout. Today's administrators are expected to have excellent IT skills and to use word-processing, spreadsheet and presentation software to produce professional-looking documents. Where staff are competent in using these types of software, businesses are able to produce documents quickly and accurately, thereby reducing time, cost and waste.

This unit follows on from Unit Q212 Produce documents in a business environment and looks at how to produce **text** using notes that you or others may have written. To demonstrate your ability to produce text from notes, you need to understand how to prepare text from notes and use IT skills to **transcribe** the notes into appropriate text or document using the right language and style. These notes may be written by you or your supervisor.

In this unit, you will look at the different types of documents that may be produced and their format. You will then examine the differences between preparing text from your notes and those written by others. The purpose and benefits of following procedures when preparing text from notes is explained, as well as the importance of agreeing the purpose, format and deadline for doing this.

As an administrator, you will need to produce documents accurately — including spelling, grammar and punctuation — and be competent in preparing text from notes professionally using IT skills. The unit describes ways of checking finished documents for accuracy and the reason for doing so. You will also investigate the reasons why documents and notes need to be stored safely and securely and the purpose of maintaining confidentiality and meeting deadlines.

The final part of the unit is a practical section that requires you to prepare text from notes. You will demonstrate your ability in inputting text using keyboard skills, format text to agreed style and layout, make efficient use of available technology, clarify text requirements when necessary, read and check texts for accuracy and finally edit and correct texts, as required.

Key terms

Text – any word-processed documents or tasks produced from notes written by you or others.

Transcribe – the process of turning handwritten notes into professionally produced documents using IT skills.

Preparing text from notes

This section links in with Unit Q212 Produce documents in a business environment. You will look at the different types of documents that may be produced and their formats and will also examine the differences between preparing text from your notes, which will enable you to overcome any difficulties when transcribing these notes.

Types of documents that may be produced from notes and appropriate formats

At work, you will be required to prepare various types of documents for different people. For example, you may be asked to prepare an agenda and notice of meeting to inform members of staff about a meeting organised for the following week. You may be required to write notes from instructions dictated by your supervisor or transcribe notes they write. Therefore, you will first have to be able to read the notes you have written or those written by your supervisor. Then you have to know the format of an agenda and notice of meeting, the appropriate language to use, make sure it is accurate and ensure participants receive the information on time.

Activity 1

Complete the table below which shows some examples of documents produced for use within the organisational (internal use) and those that are sent to customers or suppliers (external use).

Documents for internal use	Documents for external use
Email	Letter
Memorandum (memo)	Email
Notice	Brochure
Informal report	Press release

Examples of documents for internal and external use

A version of this table, ready for you to complete, is available to download from www.contentextra. com/businessadmin

Portfolio Task 213.1

→ Links to LO1: assessment criterion 1.1

Now that you know the different types of documents produced, select *five* and explain their purpose. Do this by identifying the target audience for these documents, the reason for them and provide samples to show the format or structure.

Use the table below to help you complete the evidence for this task.

Type of document	Purpose (e.g. instructions, promotion, information, etc.)	Sent to (e.g. public, staff, customers, etc.)

Functional skills

English: Reading and Writing

By professionally summarising the information in a table, you will be preparing yourself for the Reading and Writing Level 1 Functional Skills English exam. In addition, the documents you produce as evidence will reflect your Writing skills.

A version of this table, ready for you to complete, is available to download from www.contentextra. com/businessadmin

Produce text from notes Unit Q213

The difference between producing text from own notes and from others' notes

People write notes for all kinds of reasons, for example to give instructions, leave messages, make a request, pass on information (see Figure 213.1). You have probably written notes yourself — when studying, making a list of things to do, passing on telephone messages, and so on.

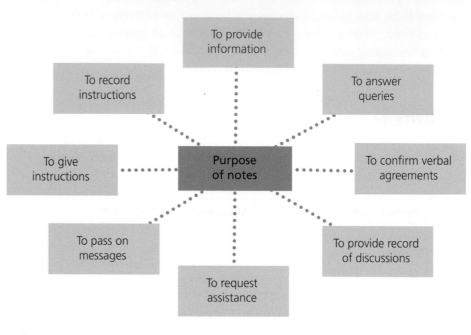

Figure 213.1: *The purpose of notes*

Writing your own notes

Use a shorthand pad or notebook to make notes, and always write neatly so that your notes are legible. Your notepad needs to be kept close at hand — either on your desk, or take it with you when seeing other people — so that you can always refer to it or add to your notes.

Notes from others

When you receive notes from others, ensure that you read through them to find out what is required. This will give you time to check with the person the purpose of the note as well as the format and type of document to be produced.

Activity 2

From your personal experience at work, think of any problems you had while trying to read notes written by other members of staff. Make a list of these.

Try reading the information in Figure 213.2.

I will be away from the office today. Pls could you arrange to complete these by 3pm and leave them on my desk:

1. Letter to Mrs Baker to arrange a mtg for Tues, 6 Oct at 9.30 am in our office

2. Type up the mins from yesterday's mtg

3. Prepare a chq for payment to the travel agent for my flight next wk

4. Distribute the magazine that I have left on your desk to the Sales Dept

Figure 213.2: *Example of handwritten note*

If you are able to read this, you have almost learned how to read from notes. Some of the difficulties that you may have identified include the use of jargon or technical language which you do not understand, abbreviations that might be difficult to spell and hand writing that may sometimes be impossible to read.

Portfolio Task 213.2 → Links to LO1: assessment criterion 1.2

Make a note of at least *three* differences between producing text from your own notes and that of others.

Can you read your notes better than those written by others? If you can, explain what the differences are between producing text using your own notes and producing text using others' notes. To help you, answer the following questions about the differences between your notes and others.

*   Was your handwriting easier to read?
*   Were you able to understand what you wrote better than notes written by others?
*   Were you able to read and understand your notes correctly?
*   Do you use abbreviations in your notes?
*   Do you understand abbreviations used by others?
*   Did you have difficulty spelling any unfamiliar words?

Present this information appropriately using your IT skills. For example, you could write an email to your tutor explaining the differences between producing text from your own notes and producing text from others' notes. Print out the email as your evidence.

Purpose and benefits of following procedures when preparing text from notes

This section will help you to understand the purpose and benefits of preparing text from notes accurately and on time using appropriate procedures. It will highlight the purpose of preparing text accurately from notes by checking them for correctness. It will also provide suggestions on how to manage text and notes safely and securely, taking confidentiality and data protection into consideration.

Benefits of agreeing the purpose, format and deadline for preparing text from notes

Before you begin typing or preparing text from notes, you will need to make sure you are clear about the purpose, format and deadline for the task. This will help to ensure that you have enough time to complete the task and to check and correct your work in order to meet the deadline.

When you are given a handwritten task, it may take time to read through and understand it. Handwritten notes are usually written quickly, so sometimes they can be difficult to read. It is important to check the purpose, format and deadline for the task straightaway since this will help you to:

- ensure that tasks are completed in time
- allow time to check and correct your work
- make sure that you are not overloaded with too much work at once
- use your resources efficiently and effectively so that work is completed correctly the first time with minimal corrections.

Portfolio Task 213.3 → Links to LO2: assessment criterion 2.1

Summarise the benefits of organising and agreeing your tasks with your supervisor by completing the table below. The first one has been done for you.

A version of this table, ready for you to complete, is available to download from www.contentextra.com/businessadmin

Benefits to the organisation	Benefits to you
• Tasks can be done on time	• Manage your time

Purpose of accuracy when preparing text from notes

Any information or documents that you prepare must be accurate since the business relies on providing correct information to its customers. For example, a **quotation** for a new service or product needs to be accurate and sent promptly to a customer to ensure that the business does not lose a potential new order. Incorrectly typed figures could mean the loss of a new customer or an order that is below cost, causing the business to lose money. When documents are accurate, it reflects on the ability of the business's staff, the quality of work they produce and their level of professionalism. This, in turn, reflects on the professionalism of the organisation itself.

Key terms

Quotation – estimate of the price of a product or service.

Proof-read – the method of checking work for grammar, spelling, punctuation as well as consistent structure and appropriate format.

Checking finished documents for accuracy and correctness

Why check documents?

When you have completed your work, what do you do? Do you have time to check it and make any corrections before giving it to your supervisor to sign? This is important as sloppy work would create a poor impression of you and the organisation and could cost the business money if information given is incorrect.

How to check documents

To make sure you produce accurate documents, you should use at least one of the following methods to check your work.

- Read it aloud to yourself so that you can hear any mistakes in grammar or punctuation.
- Use a ruler or cover to read through line by line.
- Ask a colleague to check it.
- Check each word for spelling. Then read through the whole document to make sure the content is easy to understand and accurate.

Remember to check for grammar, spelling and punctuation. When you **proof-read** text for accuracy, use a dictionary, thesaurus or other reference books to check for jargon or technical terms. Finally, for a professional image you will need to make sure that the correct format is used and presentation is consistent throughout.

When checking text for accuracy, why might it help you to refer to a dictionary, thesaurus or other reference book?

Activity 3

If your supervisor asked you to write a letter to a customer, what format would you use? Look at the sample below and list what needs to be improved.

M E M O R A N D U M

TO: Mr J Jones

FROM: Mr K Townsend

Date: 23 March 2011

REF: KC/tt

PARTICULARS OF CLAIM

Dear sir

Thank you for you rleter dated 7 March. I am writing to organise a time and date for Mrs S Smith, our Claims Officer to visit you and assess the damage the your property.

Please make sure that you have all the necessary evidence needed for us to assess your claim. Some of the evidence may be:

Photograph of the damage
Quotations for repair to the damage

I would be grateful if you could either call us on 01234 555555 or email Mrs Smith directly on ssmith@insureandgo.co.uk.

Best regards

K. Townsend

K TOWNSEND
Claims Manager

A version of this table, ready for you to complete, is available to download from www.contentextra.com/businessadmin

---

✔ Checklist

Using appropriate document structure and format

When producing your document, remember to use:

- the correct format, e.g. memo, letter or minutes
- consistent font type throughout
- a larger font size for headings, if appropriate
- consistent line spacing and paragraphing
- margins that display the document clearly.

Ways of storing text and notes safely and securely

Why store work securely?

After completing your work, you will need to store the notes and texts safely and securely. There are several reasons for this.

- You may need to refer to them to confirm arrangements agreed previously.
- They may help you to make informed decisions.
- It is your responsibility to keep customer and staff information confidential.
- It may be necessary to do so to comply with legislation.

Text and notes may be kept safe and secure using both traditional and/or electronic methods. Traditional methods include the use of lockable storage cupboards, filing cabinets or drawers as well as a safe that may be locked and alarmed. To prevent unauthorised access, only certain people may have access to the documents and notes. More modern electronic methods include computer passwords, restricted access to data and maintaining back-up data.

Purpose of confidentiality and data protection when preparing text from notes

As an administrator, you constantly deal with information that is private and confidential as it relates to the organisation's clients or employees. This data must be kept confidential and may only be used for reasons stated by the organisation in order to comply with the Data Protection Act 1998.

It is essential that you do not allow unauthorised people access to this information. Before leaving your desk, make sure that you remove any notes and documents — store them safely in a locked drawer or filing cabinet — and log off the computer system or lock your screen so that no one can access your documents while you are not around. If confidential information is leaked the business could lose its customers and reputation.

Purpose and benefits of meeting deadlines

Your work as an administrator will include producing documents to meet the needs of customers, who may be customers of the business or other members of staff. For example, you may be required to prepare an invoice. Your supervisor may have provided you with the necessary information and you would need to use the appropriate form to send to the customer. If you send the invoice late, the organisation may not be paid, or if you type the wrong amount, the business may lose money as it was underpaid. Table 213.1 lists the benefits to both the organisation and the employee of preparing accurate and timely documents.

Benefit to organisation	Benefit to employee
• Important documents will meet customers' needs	• Time to check and correct your work to maintain your own reputation
• Give enough time to correct errors	• Able to prioritise workload
• Give organisation a good reputation	• Manage workload to reduce stress

Table 213.1: *Benefits of preparing accurate and timely documents*

Portfolio Task 213.4

➜ Links to LO2: assessment criteria 2.4, 2.5 and 2.6

Use the following headings to summarise your understanding of:

- the purpose of storing text and notes safely and securely
- the methods of securing these
- the purpose of confidentiality and data protection when preparing text from notes
- the purpose and benefits of meeting deadlines.

Present the information in a booklet, using relevant IT software. Use appropriate headings and include graphics and images to make the booklet interesting.

Functional skills

English: Reading and Writing
If you are able to summarise the information in a booklet accurately and professionally, you will be preparing yourself for the Reading and Writing Level 1 Functional Skills English exam.

Prepare text from notes
Agree the purpose, format and deadlines for texts

Figure 213.3 shows the steps to be taken when preparing text from your own or others' notes.

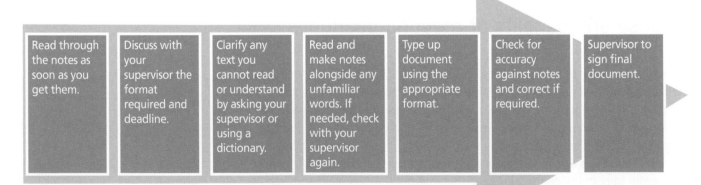

| Read through the notes as soon as you get them. | Discuss with your supervisor the format required and deadline. | Clarify any text you cannot read or understand by asking your supervisor or using a dictionary. | Read and make notes alongside any unfamiliar words. If needed, check with your supervisor again. | Type up document using the appropriate format. | Check for accuracy against notes and correct if required. | Supervisor to sign final document. |

Figure 213.3: *Steps when preparing notes*

Portfolio Task 213.5

→ Links to LO2: assessment criteria 2.2 and 2.3; LO3: assessment criterion 3.1

Using Figure 213.3, complete the log sheet below to show how you agreed the purpose, format and deadline for documents you produced from notes you and others wrote. The documents themselves will form part of the evidence for portfolio task 213.6.

Purpose, e.g. giving information, promotion, etc.	Format of text completed from notes, e.g. memo, letter, email, etc.	Deadline agreed with supervisor	Name of supervisor for the task

When you have completed the table, add the information below.

- Explain why you need to produce accurate text from notes (including the need for accurate spelling, grammar and punctuation).

- Describe ways you used to check the finished documents for accuracy and correctness, and why you need to proof-read your work.

Functional skills

English: Reading and Writing

If you are able to summarise your research effectively and professionally, you will be preparing yourself for the Reading and Writing Level 1 Functional Skills English exam.

A version of this table, ready for you to complete, is available to download from the website.

Office life

Nina's story

My name is Nina Field. I'm 19 and have recently started work as an administrative assistant in the Housing Office at the local council. I'm also completing my Business Administration apprenticeship there.

One of my responsibilities is to deal with telephone messages received through the centralised phone system. I listen to the messages, write them down and then find out from my supervisor how to deal with them. My supervisor often leaves me handwritten messages with the day's work to be completed by 4 pm in time for her signature and the post.

Ask the expert

Q On an average day, I will have at least 15 telephone messages to deal with. My supervisor also leaves me a handwritten message with 5–10 tasks that I am expected to complete by the end of the day. My supervisor's writing can be very difficult to read, and if I've written down something in a hurry, I can't always read my own notes. When I have too much to do, I often leave some of my tasks to the next day. Sometimes, I have so many pieces of paper on my desk that I have lost messages. I'm just not sure where to start – how can I complete as many tasks as possible in a day?

A Write your notes in a notebook so you can refer to them later.
- You may find it helpful to keep a log of the work that you complete in a day. This will show your supervisor the amount of work you complete daily and the time you need to complete different tasks.
- Using this log, you will be able to allocate time to complete the work. For example, you could allocate the first hour of the day to listening to and distributing telephone messages. Then, you could deal with your supervisor's message. After lunch, you could deal with the telephone messages received that morning. At the end of each day, you should make a list of things that you may have to complete for the next day.
- With a record of your responsibilities written in a log, you will be able to identify any training needs. For example, training to achieve a typing speed of 40 wpm will make you more efficient and effective.

Top tips

Improve your ability to produce text from notes accurately and efficiently by following these tips:
- Read through the notes first to get an idea of what is required. Ask your supervisor if you can't read her writing.
- Discuss the format and deadline for the task with your supervisor.
- Decide on the structure and arrangement of paragraphs or headings.
- Make sure you have enough time to complete the task and check it for spelling (using a dictionary), punctuation, grammar and format.
- Correct the work before the deadline if possible, so that you will have time to make any changes that your supervisor might identify.

Evidence collection

In order for you to complete the assessment criteria for learning outcome 4, you will need to provide evidence of at least *four* relevant documents produced from notes to show that you have demonstrated the required skills and competence to do so within agreed deadlines. (You may like to use Figure 213.4 to help you complete the tasks step-by-step.)

Evidence can be collected in a number of different ways. For example, it can be either a signed witness testimony from a colleague or line manager or a log sheet showing the types of documents produced from written notes with copies of these documents and the notes.

Prepare text from notes

This section will help you to check on your ability to prepare text from notes using appropriate IT technology and keyboard skills. You should be able to prepare the necessary text using agreed style and layout, check for any unfamiliar words, read and check text for accuracy and correct these as required. This must be completed within agreed deadlines.

Portfolio Task 213.6	→ Links to LO4: assessment criteria 4.1, 4.2, 4.3, 4.4, 4.5, 4.6 and 4.7	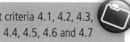

Using the log sheet you produced in portfolio task 213.5, provide evidence of completed tasks together with the instruction notes or drafts.

Write a summary of your organisational procedure for storing text and notes securely and safely. Document your evidence using screen shots or photographs, if you prefer.

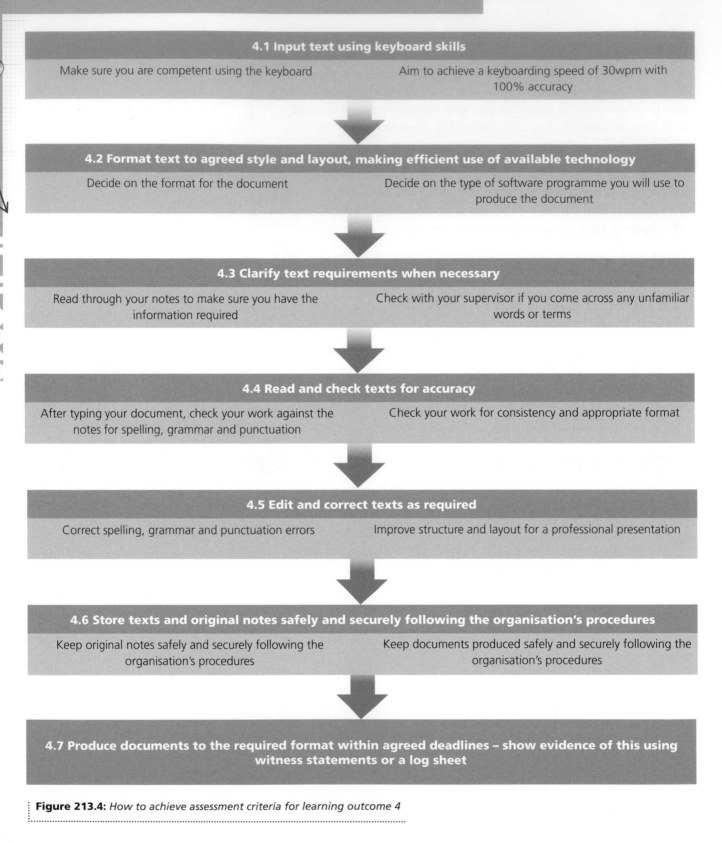

4.1 Input text using keyboard skills

Make sure you are competent using the keyboard

Aim to achieve a keyboarding speed of 30wpm with 100% accuracy

4.2 Format text to agreed style and layout, making efficient use of available technology

Decide on the format for the document

Decide on the type of software programme you will use to produce the document

4.3 Clarify text requirements when necessary

Read through your notes to make sure you have the information required

Check with your supervisor if you come across any unfamiliar words or terms

4.4 Read and check texts for accuracy

After typing your document, check your work against the notes for spelling, grammar and punctuation

Check your work for consistency and appropriate format

4.5 Edit and correct texts as required

Correct spelling, grammar and punctuation errors

Improve structure and layout for a professional presentation

4.6 Store texts and original notes safely and securely following the organisation's procedures

Keep original notes safely and securely following the organisation's procedures

Keep documents produced safely and securely following the organisation's procedures

4.7 Produce documents to the required format within agreed deadlines – show evidence of this using witness statements or a log sheet

Figure 213.4: *How to achieve assessment criteria for learning outcome 4*

Check your knowledge

1 Which of the following is not a document prepared for an external customer?

   a. Letter.

   b. Memo.

   c. Quotation.

   d. Promotional leaflet.

2 Which of these document(s) may be distributed among staff members?

   a. Memo.

   b. Telephone message.

   c. Press release.

   d. Letter.

3 Which of the following is not a method of proof-reading?

   a. Reading a document aloud to yourself.

   b. Asking a colleague to read your work.

   c. Typing the work.

   d. Using a ruler to check your work line by line.

4 Why would you produce text from notes?

   a. To provide a quotation.

   b. To type up a verbal discussion.

   c. To give information.

   d. To promote the business.

5 Which are the area(s) that need to be checked when preparing text from notes?

   a. Grammar.

   b. Punctuation.

   c. Format.

   d. Spelling.

6 Which of the following are problem(s) that you may face when reading notes written by others?

   a. Some of the words used are too technical.

   b. Cannot understand what is written because of poor handwriting.

   c. Cannot spell some abbreviations used.

   d. Cannot spell unfamiliar words.

7 Which of the following is a method of checking work for grammar, spelling, punctuation and format?

   a. Reading.

   b. Comprehension.

   c. Proof-reading.

   d. Transcribing.

8 Which of these are traditional method(s) for storing text and notes?

   a. Locked filing cabinets.

   b. Electronic files.

   c. Locked drawers.

   d. Secure passwords.

9 Which of these is an electronic method of safely storing text?

   a. A safe.

   b. Locked filing cabinets.

   c. Locked drawers.

   d. Secure passwords.

10 Which of these statement(s) identifies the benefits of meeting deadlines to the organisation?

   a. To meet the needs of both internal and external customers.

   b. To allow staff to prioritise and manage their time.

   c. To help the organisation to maintain and improve its reputation for being reliable.

   d. To enable the organisation to manage its time and resources efficiently and effectively.

Answers to these questions can be found on www.contentextra.com/businessadmin

What your assessor is looking for

Each unit in this qualification comprises two types of assessment requirements. These are:

- knowledge-based learning outcomes
- performance indicators.

In order to prepare for and succeed in completing this unit, your assessor will require you to be able to demonstrate competence in all of the performance criteria listed in the table below.

Your assessor will guide you through the assessment process, but it is likely that for this unit you will need to:

- complete short written narratives or personal statements explaining your answers
- take part in professional discussions with your assessor to explain your answers verbally
- complete observations with your assessor ensuring that they can observe you carrying out your work tasks

- produce any relevant work products to help demonstrate how you have completed the assessment criteria
- ask your manager, a colleague or a customer for witness testimonies explaining how you have completed the assessment criteria.

The evidence which you generate for the assessment criteria in this unit may also count towards your evidence collection for some of the other units in this qualification. Your assessor will provide support and guidance on this.

The table below outlines the portfolio tasks which you need to complete for this unit, mapped to their associated performance criteria, knowledge and, where appropriate, functional skills.

Task and page reference	Mapping assessment criteria
Portfolio task 213.1 (page 197)	Assessment criterion: 1.1
Portfolio task 213.2 (page 199)	Assessment criterion: 1.2
Portfolio task 213.3 (page 200)	Assessment criterion: 2.1
Portfolio task 213.4 (page 204)	Assessment criteria: 2.4, 2.5, 2.6
Portfolio task 213.5 (page 205)	Assessment criteria: 2.2, 2.3, 3.1
Portfolio task 213.6 (page 207)	Assessment criteria: 4.1, 4.2, 4.3, 4.4, 4.5, 4.6, 4.7

Glossary

Absenteeism – employee absence from work.

Accountable – to be responsible for something.

Allegation – an accusation against someone.

Annual performance review – a meeting between an employee and their manager to discuss the employee's work performance over the past year and set work-related targets for the forthcoming year.

Appraisal system – one-to-one discussions that are held privately between a supervisor or manager and individual staff to review progress, performance and responsibilities. The process may take place annually or twice a year and gives employees the chance to talk about their achievements and identify areas that they want to develop. Appraisal should be a two-way process where information is shared and plans made for the employee's future development.

Automation – using machines and computers, instead of people, to complete tasks.

Back-stabbing – where an individual is rude about a colleague, or takes action behind their back that may be harmful to them.

Benchmark – standard by which performance can be measured, usually set in terms of quality, cost and time.

Boom – a high point in terms of output and growth in the economy, where businesses are doing well, people are well off and have money to spend.

Capital investment – money spent on items such as buildings, machinery, equipment and land. These are long-term purchases which will help the business to make money.

Carbon footprint – the amount of carbon dioxide (CO_2) being produced by a business or individual.

Career progression – the jobs you will move on to later in your working life.

Client – customer of a business. A client can be either an individual or another business.

Client relationship – the relationship between a company and a client (the customer). Companies always try to maintain very good relationships with their clients in order to do future business with them.

Collate – to collect together and analyse.

Constructive feedback – feedback given to staff based on areas for improvement. It may not always be about negative issues and is intended to be honest feedback without being personal. To be constructive, feedback must be timely and provide solutions to help someone improve.

Continuous professional development (CPD) – employees are encouraged to continuously learn and improve their skills and knowledge to be more competitive in the workplace. They are usually required to keep a record of this through the organisation's appraisal system, by updating their CV or keeping records of their qualifications/awards.

Corporate – of the company.

Cost base – the very basic costs to keep a business running, such as wages, heating, lighting, water and rent.

Cost/benefit analysis – a report which demonstrates the benefits of something relative to its costs. The aim is to show that it is worth the cost, as it will provide many benefits to the business.

Culture – the usual way in which things are done in a company and the general feeling of the workplace. A culture develops slowly over years and cannot be changed overnight.

Customer relationship management (CRM) database – special type of database which stores detailed information about a business's customers (including their purchase history and even their birthday and children's names) so that products and services can be tailored to their individual needs and wants.

Deadline – the date by which a task must be done.

Director – a senior manager who is elected by the shareholders to make decisions and run the company on their behalf.

Disciplinary action – a set of procedures which a business will follow when taking action against staff if they fail to carry out their duties properly, or commit certain offences at work.

Discounted price – where the original price of the item has been lowered.

Discrimination – when someone is treated unfairly on the basis of their ethnic origin, religion, age, sexual orientation, gender or ability.

Diverse team — a group of people who possess different skills, personality traits and attributes which, when combined together as part of a team, support the team's goals as a whole.

Diversification — a business strategy to increase profits by entering new markets and selling new products.

Dividend — a share of the company's profits. This is the reward that a shareholder receives.

Draft — an early version of a document that is still in the process of being checked for accuracy.

Efficiency — the speed and the quality of work. A task completed efficiently is one that is done quickly and to a good standard.

Email audit trail — a record of all the emails sent and received that can be used as evidence of discussion and agreement.

Empathy — being able to appreciate how someone else might be feeling, and why they might be feeling this way.

Employment legislation — special laws relating to work.

Ethical — having certain standards or principles. For example, The Body Shop attempts to carry out its business without causing harm to people, animals or the planet.

Expertise — a very high level of skills in a certain area.

External client — a customer who works for another organisation.

Finite resources — non-renewable supplies such as metals, oil, coal and gas which will run out eventually.

Formal meeting — usually involves following a prepared set of questions. The meeting may include more senior managers and opportunities to speak freely will probably be limited.

Franchise — a person or company who has brought the local rights to use the name, logo and brand image of another company.

Franchisor — the holder of the franchise who will sell the rights to use their name, logo and brand image to a franchisee in return for a share of the profit.

Headed paper — paper that has the company's logo and contact details printed at the top.

Incentive — something, such as a cash bonus, that motivates people to achieve higher results.

Industry body — organisation set up to monitor and regulate the activities of its members. For example, the UK's regional water companies are regulated by the Office of Water Services (Ofwat), which ensures that they act in accordance with its rules and regulations on water quality and prices.

Inefficiencies — aspects of a business that are generally wasteful, use to many resources or do not produce the desired results, for example, outdated machines that run slowly and break down regularly, or processes that take too long to complete.

Informal meeting — often takes the form of a general discussion about how well the employee has done in their work. The employee is likely to have freedom to express their thoughts and feelings openly.

Job description — an outline of the job title, aims of the job, name of the supervisor and duties, usually written by the employee's manager.

Key performance targets — targets setting out what staff should achieve in their work.

Legislation — laws passed by the government.

Line manager — the person to whom you report at work. Your line manager is usually the person who gives you your work and sets the deadlines for your work.

Mailshots — marketing letters sent out by a company to people on a mailing list.

Mentor — trusted guide or adviser.

Motivation — the reason or incentive for an individual or group choosing to make a particular decision.

Multinational — a company that operates in more than one country.

Norm — the normal way in which things are done.

Noxious chemical residue — unpleasant and harmful chemicals left over at the end of a production process.

Outsourcing — giving a task or function to another company to perform for you.

Overspend — occurs when a project costs more than the planned budget.

Ownership — taking responsibility for something and having a willingness to work towards it.

Person specification — lists the types of qualification, skills and qualities of the person for the job, usually written by the employee's manager.

Philosophy — a belief or a set of values.

Productivity — the rate at which a person works. The more productive you are, the more you will achieve.

Profit — the amount of money left over from a company's sales revenue once costs have been taken away (profit = revenue − costs).

Proofread – the method of checking work for grammar, spelling, punctuation as well as consistent structure and appropriate format.

Proprietary – something that is owned by a company and is not free for the public to use.

Quality circles – groups of workers who meet together to discuss how to make improvements to their working methods to produce better results.

Quotation – estimate of the price of a product or service.

Realistic target – a task that can be completed within the time given.

Recession – a downturn in the economy, where businesses are not doing well and people do not have much money to spend.

Redeployment – moving staff from one part of the organisation to work in another part. This is done in order to make the business more efficient.

Redundancy – when a business no longer requires staff and they lose their jobs.

Resources – office equipment, meeting room facilities, computers, faces, telephones – any and all of the things you need in order to do your job.

Revenue – money coming in to the business as a result of sales of its products and services.

Share – a part of the business.

Shareholder – a part owner of a company.

Skills audit – the process of measuring existing staff's qualifications and skills against the skills, knowledge and experience required for the future.

Skills gaps – the difference between the skills an employee has and those required to carry out a job.

Staff morale – how happy the staff are. High morale means they are happy and low morale means they ware unhappy.

Staff retention – a measure of the number of people who leave a company each year. If staff retention is high, the company is retaining (keeping) most of its staff; if it is low, many people are leaving.

Staff turnover – the number of people who leave a company over a year, usually expressed as a percentage.

Stakeholder – any person or organisation who has an interest in the activities of a business.

Stock – supplies which a business keeps for future use and can include the raw materials to be used in the manufacture of products.

Strapline – a short, catchy phrase that a company will use to help strengthen its brand identity with customers.

Strategic business plan – a plan for the long term, usually five years, which views the business as a whole.

Streamlined – working practices that have been refined and made as efficient as possible.

Succession planning – process of identifying internal staff to prepare and develop them for more responsible senior jobs/positions.

Support functions – including marketing, human resources, IT sales and accounts.

Surplus – the money left over from donations once the charity has paid its expenses.

Sustainable – something that can continue for the foreseeable future.

Task force – a special, expert team brought together to complete a specific task.

Team productivity – the output of the team per day or per week. Teams tend to be more productive than individuals as they are able to motivate each other.

Text – any word-processed documents or tasks produced from notes written by you or others.

Trade credit – a system for payment when a business takes the goods, and then pays for them at a later, agreed date (buy now, pay later).

Transcribe – the process of turning handwritten notes into professionally produced documents using IT skills.

Transferable skills – special skills, such as problem solving, which are useful in all jobs.

Unique selling point (USP) – the feature(s) of a product or organisation that makes it different from its competitors.

Variance – difference.

Variance analysis – a comparison of the budgeted figures with the actual costs that were incurred. This is carried out to see if there were any differences between the two sets of figures and to identify the reasons for this.

Wastage – waste caused by business processes such as manufacturing.

Working conditions – the work environment, such as safety, hygiene, hours of work, break times and even possibilities of advancement.

Workload – the tasks which you need to complete

Index

Key terms are indicated by **bold** page numbers.